Dave & LaJean,

Thank you for you interest in my book. It will be one of encouragement, inspiration and one of faith-building.

God bless,
Bud

Bud Kolstad
4/28/19

Live ready!
LK 21:36

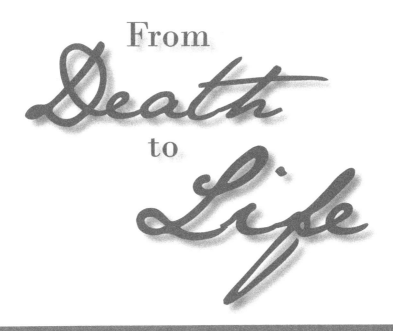

From *Death* to *Life*

MY JOURNEY THROUGH CANCER

*"I will not die, but live, and declare the works
and recount the illustrious acts of the Lord."*

**BUD KOLSTAD
JILL CROMWELL**

ISBN 978-1-64416-615-4 (paperback)
ISBN 978-1-64416-617-8 (hardcover)
ISBN 978-1-64416-616-1 (digital)

Copyright © 2018 by Bud Kolstad and Jill Cromwell

All rights reserved. No part of this publication may be reproduced, distributed, or transmitted in any form or by any means, including photocopying, recording, or other electronic or mechanical methods without the prior written permission of the publisher. For permission requests, solicit the publisher via the address below.

Christian Faith Publishing, Inc.
832 Park Avenue
Meadville, PA 16335
www.christianfaithpublishing.com

Scriptures marked KJV are taken from the KING JAMES VERSION (KJV): KING JAMES VERSION, public domain.

Unless otherwise indicated, all Scripture quotations are taken from the Holy Bible, New Living Translation, copyright © 1996, 2004, 2015 by Tyndale House Foundation. Used by permission of Tyndale House Publishers, Inc., Carol Stream, Illinois 60188. All rights reserved.

Scripture quotations marked (NIV) are taken from the Holy Bible, New International Version®, NIV®. Copyright © 1973, 1978, 1984, 2011 by Biblica, Inc.™ Used by permission of Zondervan. All rights reserved worldwide. www.zondervan.com The "NIV" and "New International Version" are trademarks registered in the United States Patent and Trademark Office by Biblica, Inc.™

Cover Design by Lyndsay Martin

Printed in the United States of America

To my Lord and Savior, Jesus Christ. Without His guidance throughout my life and the miracle He brought about recorded in this book, I would not have a reason nor the ability to write the following narrative. From death to life, on three separate occasions, He has sustained me and shown me who He is in a brand-new light. He deserves all the praise, honor, and glory due His name.

Secondly, I would like to recognize the doctors and nurses that took excellent care of me during my six months in the Veterans Hospital in Seattle, Washington. Their daily sacrifice, as they served my needs and helped me through the most difficult time in my life, is much appreciated. They do not get the praise they deserve, and I want to make it known that they are the heroes in my opinion.

Thirdly, without the help of Jill Cromwell, this book would not have the smooth story line that you will follow with ease. I had the facts, but Jill put them into an interesting, uncomplicated, and emotionally charged format. In my opinion, she is one of the up-and-coming superstars in the chirography profession.

CONTENTS

Foreword 7
Preface 9
Acknowledgments 11
Introduction 15
Chapter 1: The Backstory 23
Chapter 2: God's Timing 31
Chapter 3: Working for Our Good 39
Chapter 4: The Journey Begins 46
Chapter 5: A Miraculous Provision 52
Chapter 6: When Plans Change 58
Chapter 7: A New Place of Trust 64
Chapter 8: God's Healing Power 71
Chapter 9: On the Outside Looking In 83
Chapter 10: Assignment Canceled 91
Chapter 11: A New Day Has Dawned 98
Chapter 12: Faith Matters 105
Chapter 13: A New Release 112
Chapter 14: A Much-Needed Break 121
Chapter 15: God is Relentless Too 127
Chapter 16: Knocked Down but Not Defeated 134
Chapter 17: Not Out of the Woods 143
Chapter 18: Blessings in a Crisis 150
Chapter 19: We're Almost There 154
Chapter 20: In Honor of the Caregiver 161
Chapter 21: Welcome Home 166
Chapter 22: From Spiritual Death to Spiritual Life 172
Appendix 181

FOREWORD

One rainy Sunday morning, a couple walked through the doors of our church. They were notably energetic and full of life and passion. They were the type of individuals that every pastor dreams of having in their church—people who love Jesus, love people, are eager to serve in any way possible, and always have an encouraging word. That couple was Bud and Melody Kolstad, and they fit that description perfectly.

As I got to know them more, I was amazed to hear of Bud's story of life, challenges, death, and resurrection. I would never have guessed that the man walking through those church doors on that Sunday morning had faced so many challenges in his life and was literally a walking miracle!

> *James 1:2–4 Consider it pure joy, my brothers and sisters whenever you face trials of many kinds, because you know that the testing of your faith produces perseverance. Let perseverance finish its work so that you may be mature and complete, not lacking anything. (NIV)*

God has taken Bud and Melody on a journey of trials of many kinds, and God has and is producing something great in their lives. As you read this book, I pray that you will be encouraged by God's faithfulness and that your faith will be strengthened as you believe for miracles in your own life's trials.

Blessings!

—Pastor Andy Rosas
Riverview Community Church

PREFACE

I first connected with Bud Kolstad because of our mutual desire to keep growing in our walks with God. We meet each week to read large blocks of the Bible and share what God is teaching us. You would think after reading *From Death to Life* that Bud doesn't need to grow any more in his faith. To the contrary, he hungers for more and more of Jesus. This book is a testimony of God's multiple miracles in his life, but in particular, victory over aggressive cancer and death.

I have the privilege of witnessing Bud's life as an *"open-book"* every week. I can assure you, he is the same person you will find in this book. His life is full of miracles and excitement. While it is said that our life will eventually be summarized in one sentence, Bud is an exception. He is a teacher. He is a prayer warrior with a list that requires hours of prayer every day. He is a disciple-maker. But in the end, Bud inspires me. He inspires my faith to put more trust in a loving God. To persevere. If you need hope and inspiration, this is the book for you.

Randall Hoag
President of Vision of Community Fellowship

ACKNOWLEDGMENTS

The following are family members represented in this book.

Melody is my wife. I call her my "angel." She is totally committed to Jesus and His will, without reservation. She promised to take me for better, for worse, and many times, she got the worse. Melody took me for richer, for poorer, and many times as my partner in this life, she received the "poorer." In sickness and in health, once again, too much of the time there was sickness, as this book will bear out. Although many times I didn't deserve it, she promised to love and to cherish, till death do us part. This book will tell how she followed me and stood beside me all the way to death.

Shawna is my daughter, a very kind, compassionate, and giving person. She would drop everything she had going if she thought I needed her help, as you will read later in this book.

Her brother, Gabe, wrote, "Shawna is a world-changer. She probably doesn't realize it, but she is a leader who makes so many people's lives better. When most of us see a need and keep walking, Shawna has organized her life around helping people through hard times. She has courageously decided to take setbacks, difficulties, and pain, then recycle them into acts of love and understanding. She models compassion to her family and friends; she gives generously to those in need; and she serves people consistently in her work and play. Growing up, I always knew Shawna was bound for something great, and it's a joy to watch her live out her God-given calling so well. While we had a few years of disconnection and distance, our adulthood has brought us close as friends and siblings, and now even neighbors. I wouldn't have it any other way. I love you Shawna!"

Gabe is my son. Gabe, too, is a very giving person, one who has a shepherd's heart as a Pastor of a church in Beaverton, Oregon. He is a person of unbelievable integrity who can be depended on to tell the truth, no matter if it is painful or not at the time. His Godly wisdom is immeasurable.

His sister, Shawna, wrote, "Gabe has always been there for me no matter what. Even when I strayed away from the Lord in my early adulthood, he never stopped being a support for me, and he never ever judged me. I believe the grace he showed me was a big part of my coming back to the Lord. When I struggled with divorce from my first husband, he was there. He went to the courthouse with me to file a restraining order. He made me feel safe.

"When I was a single mom and trying to stay afloat, he and Melissa were there for me. They watched Hayden for me when I couldn't afford childcare. They made me feel like I wasn't alone. When I met my current husband, he was there to celebrate with me in my newfound love. He made me feel supported.

"When our two-year-old son was diagnosed with cancer, he wept with us and supported us in many ways. He made us feel loved. With the birth of each of my children, he beamed with pride to be their uncle. He made me feel proud.

"He gives honest advice and great support any time I need or want it. Gabe has been consistent in my life, and honestly, I don't know where I'd be without him and Melissa. They're not only my brother and sister-in-law but two of my best friends, and I'm so very thankful for them."

Jackie is my older sister. She has been beside me no matter what the circumstance, without condemnation, and yet with all the praise one could give. Jackie has been a great friend to me dating back to childhood.

Jill wrote about her, "Jackie has always been '*the heart*' of our family. While growing up, and being the oldest of four siblings, her attention and care was always directed toward my brothers' and my well-being. When she got her first job, her thoughts were what she could buy for us, or our mom and dad. This carried through, even after she got married. She is the most thoughtful and caring person I know. She will give you her heart, not taking into consideration that she might get hurt or taken advantage of. She will listen, comfort, encourage, and forgive you, over and over again. She truly cares about others, and her heart will help carry your burdens, feel your pain, and stay with you through the end. She is someone you can trust, no matter what you need, because she truly has a heart filled with love.

"You won't find her in big crowds, or in the forefront. She likes to stay hidden in the background so as not to be noticed. But in any situation, you will feel her love, see her pure heart, and hear her laughter. She will always be there for you.

"God blessed me with the most wonderful sister I could have ever wished for but then went above and beyond by giving me a sister who would be one of my closest and best friends."

Bruce is my younger brother who has been my best friend, not including Jesus and Melody. We have been very close from our youth. We have had the brotherly relationship all brothers should have.

An added note from Linda, His wife, "I count it a privilege to be married to Bruce. Bruce is the most godly man I know, always seeking what the Lord would have us to do and searching for lost souls to reach out to, boldly in fact. His goal in life is to do God's will, in his life and ours together. He's the love of my life, always doing whatever he can to make me feel like a queen, always putting me first, and never wanting anything for himself. He is the most awesome Father and Grandfather, the envy of most. He is a comedian on the side and always makes me laugh; he's giving, generous, and loving, and I'm so thankful that God has allowed me to travel this journey on earth with him.

Linda is Bruce's wife. Linda is not only my sister-in-law but a very good friend to me. She is a wonderful sister-in-law, loyal, supporting, and one who is willing to go the extra mile in any instance she is needed.

Bruce writes, "Linda is a very strong, loving, reliable, giving, and faithful person. She truly loves the Lord, and it shows in her daily life. She is very protective of her family and will do anything to protect them. A great mother and grandmother who devotes much of her prayer time to her kids and grandkids even when they are unaware she's doing it. She can always be counted on in a time of crisis, ready to spend time in prayer or to offer a hand. She would give everything she owns if I would let her and is a faithful friend to those close to her. I can't imagine having a better friend, confidant, and companion to spend my life with. If there is no marriage in Heaven, then Linda and I will have to be Siamese Twins since we are inseparable. Linda is the love and joy of my heart. Oh! What a blessed man I am!"

Jill is my younger sister, a lady who lives exactly what she preaches. She was the person that made a journal of my story, which you will read in later chapters. She is one of the most amazing people I know on this earth.

My older sister, Jackie, wrote, "Jill is so easy to write about. When I was nine years old, Mom told us she was going to have a baby. I was so excited, and the first words, I'm sure, was I want a sister. On June 4, 1957, my wish came true. Our Jill Elaine was born. Fast forward until now, God blessed me with the best sister I could ever have. There have been ups and downs, especially in her teenage years, but God came into her life and completely changed her. She's always been there for me. Her words were so comforting and just what I needed. Her love for her Lord shines through her. She is a great prayer warrior. I get a hold of her whenever I have a prayer request, *and I know*, that as soon as we hang up, she goes to the Lord with my request. God blessed me with the best sister in the world. I love her more than anything!"

Without these voices, this book would not have been possible. That is the reason I am including each of them as I give them the greatest acknowledgment I possibly can.

INTRODUCTION

It had been less than fifteen minutes since the 8:00 p.m. shift change, the evening of January 20, 2015, at the VA hospital. One month earlier, I'd turned sixty-five and had already been enjoying my retirement of four years. Life seemed normal.

I felt healthy and could do whatever I wanted, whenever I wanted. I spent most days walking along the marina and talking to God. My relationship with Him grew immensely during this time, as He used many illustrations on the beach to teach me. I called these new lessons, modern-day parables. I looked forward to our mornings together, always in wonder of what He was going to share with me next.

I also had the freedom to do other things as well. I could go get a Starbucks if I wanted, and many days, I did. I could go to the community center and visit with other people, read the newspaper, or exercise. It was a great life that had provided me with so many new experiences and comforts beyond all my expectations. Retirement had been good.

But things began to go awry on that Friday night, January 16, that would rock my world. Life as I had known it would never be the same. Just three days earlier, on January 12, I had gone to the ER at the VA hospital. I was having an extremely difficult time breathing, so they did some tests and found my lungs were filling with fluid, and I was starting to drown in those fluids. They immediately started the process of draining the fluids and admitted me into the hospital in order to keep a close eye on how my lungs were functioning.

That led to the testing of the fluids and revealed that I now had a fast-growing form of cancer. They continued to drain my lungs for the next three days, while they immediately scheduled me for an intense chemotherapy treatment that would begin on Friday.

The chemotherapy treatment began, and for some reason, caused a disaster in my body. I was immediately taken to the ICU Department. I was thrown into a mental state of confusion and panic.

Where was I? Why was I lying in a hospital bed? How had I ended up there, and where was Melody? Confusion overwhelmed me, and I began freaking out. I'm not the kind of person that gets scared or worried when an emergency arises, as I usually go into a very focused mode. But here I was, feeling all these emotions, and I couldn't seem to get them under control. It was cold, and I was very confused. Melody, who is normally very close to me at all times, and I looked around, and she wasn't there.

It wasn't long before I heard a female voice at the end of the intensive care unit. She asked the male nurse if she could see me. This was the same nurse that I had seen at the front desk of the admissions department downstairs when I was admitted to the hospital.

The admitting attendant, a young blonde girl who was very friendly with a bubbly personality, was allowed to come in and see me in my room. Once again, she was very cordial. She asked me how I was doing, and I said that I was doing okay but that I was very tired and confused. After finishing the short conversation, she told me she'd heard I had been transferred to the ICU and wanted to come and see how I was doing.

She asked what happened, and I told her I didn't know. I asked her where I was, and again, she reiterated that I was in the ICU. We chatted for a few more minutes and then she left.

It was at that time I heard a male nurse say in a gruffly voice, "Now we'll have to get rid of her too." By this time, I was feeling really confused as to what was going on. What did he mean?

It wasn't long before, two security guards entered the nurse's station and began speaking with the head male nurse. I could hear them talking softly, but I couldn't make out what was being said. I could hear one of the guards say, "I'm not going to do it again." His voice raised and continued, "I've done it too many times, and I'm not going to do it again." There was a short time of arguing, followed by the two guards walking out. It was difficult for me to understand exactly what was happening.

The male nurse, who seemed to be the one in charge, turned to a couple of the other nurses, one male and a couple of females, and said, "Now what are we going to do?" I didn't know why or what this was all about, but my interest was on full alert. They seemed to be stunned and a bit scared. I was already wary as I had remembered them saying "they would have to get rid of her too," speaking of the nurse from downstairs. What did that mean?

It was cold, as it always is in a hospital, and I was tired, not to mention even more confused than before. With all that had just transpired, I was trying to make some sense of it. I had an IV in my arm and an oxygen tube in my nostrils which made me very uncomfortable. And as usual, when I got chilled, I asked for a warm blanket. One of the female nurses left, and I was hoping she was going to accommodate my request. Sure enough, just a few minutes later, she returned with the warm blanket and covered me. I always loved that first feeling of warmth that wrapped itself around my body when they laid the covering over me.

About thirty minutes had passed, when another security guard came in, and the same male nurse that was in charge began talking to him. Once again, their voices lowered, and I couldn't make out exactly what was being said. I assumed that the male nurse had picked up where he left off, when speaking with the other two security guards.

All of a sudden, I heard the guard say that he would need eight hundred dollars in cash to finish the job. He was told that "the job" had to be done by five-thirty the next morning. My mind began to race, and I was interpreting all this to mean that they were going to kill the admitting attendant from downstairs. But why? She had only come up to see me and find out how I was doing. Evidently, she must have heard that I was not in good shape. And as a caring hospital employee, she wanted to make sure that everything was going good for me. Shortly after I was admitted to the hospital, I went through a traumatic event where my lungs, kidneys, and heart had all stopped at the same time. Here I was, lying in a hospital bed with an IV tube injected into my arm. I was obviously sedated, and everything was happening so fast, I couldn't keep up. I was just trying to make sense of the things that I was hearing. What was going on? My mind was racing.

I heard the security guard say, "Thank you," and that's when he left. It seemed to me an exchange had taken place, and he had received the eight hundred dollars in cash. Now, he was leaving, but I couldn't figure out why.

Time slowly dragged on, and there was a lot of chatter between all the nurses in the ICU station throughout that evening. Just like before, I wasn't able to make out what was being said because they had lowered their voices. I strained, trying desperately to hear what they were saying, but to no avail.

I was feeling exhausted, yet at the same time, I was wide awake. I had become very thirsty and needed some water, so I called for a nurse. It didn't take long, and a very courteous nurse came into my room. I politely asked her if I could have some more water. She acknowledged my request with a nod, left my room, and was soon back with some fresh, cold water. She didn't stay to take vitals or visit; she just hurriedly left.

Later that evening, I was startled by the sound of a gunshot. My first thought was, "Did someone drop something?" My next thought was a little more frightening. "Was that a firecracker or was that actually a gunshot?" Now, my insides were beginning to quiver. I became anxious, thinking that "the job" they had been speaking of, concerning the administrative attendant, had just, been completed. I felt myself going into a panic mode, yet there was nothing I could do about it.

As I lay in my bed, unable to move, more questions were coming to mind, like "Why her?" "Why was it so important that she would have to die?" I had just begun trying to wrap my mind around everything that was going on when I heard the most frightening words I could have ever imagined. "He will have to be gone by then too," meaning, that I would be dead by five-thirty the next morning, along with her.

Now, extreme panic set in. It was never made known to me why they were out to eliminate me. I hadn't done anything to any of them. I had never met any of them. Unanswered questions invaded my mind. It was getting late in the evening, and I should have been going to sleep, but there was no way I could relax enough to fall asleep. I needed to know what had just happened and why, exactly, they were planning to eliminate me. I had to stay awake. I had to be alert so I could hear what they were saying. I lay in my hospital bed, listening to every word that was being spoken, in hopes that something would soon be revealed to me. I needed clarity.

The next thing I heard was the male nurse's voice. He was telling two of the female nurses that there would be calls coming in, and family members would be asking questions about "him," and again, I assumed that meant me. He told them that they needed to make it sound as if they were emotionally affected by the event. As he spoke, he kept looking into my room, as if he didn't care that I could hear him. In fact, it was as though he wanted me to know what was going on.

I kept listening intensely, trying to focus so I could hear and understand every word he was telling the nurses. I heard him instruct them that when the phone calls began coming in, they were to tell the caller how very sorry they were, but nothing could be done, that they had done everything in their power to save "him," but "he didn't make it." For the first time, full-fledged fear set in. I felt totally helpless. I couldn't even try to escape; I was trapped by tubing, plus I was in such a swollen state from medications that I could barely move.

In just a short time, the first call came through, and I could hear the nurse, her voice cracking as though she was going to burst into tears at any moment, telling the person on the other end that I had passed away. Her voice sounded very authentic and actually sounded like she really was shaken by what had happened. Just as instructed, she told the caller that my things could be picked up that morning and that she was very sorry for her loss.

I assumed the nurse had been talking to my wife, Melody, since she kept very close tabs on me and my condition during this time. Although my wife had to care for her mother at home, she spent as much time with me as possible while I was in the hospital, but she slept at home during the nights. Melody would normally return in the morning to check on me and see how I was doing.

In my mind, I was just starting to put the last phone call together when I heard another ringing of the phone, and I shuttered, hoping it wasn't another family member. Again, the same response was given to the caller. I instantly got sick to my stomach. My insides began to quiver. My mind could only imagine who this might be. I couldn't hold the tears back as I was trying to envision how the family would respond to the news that I had passed away, when in fact, I was still alive. How could I get the message to them? I was crying out in my mind. I was becoming frantic. I didn't know what to do! Another call came in, and the same rhetoric. Now, who could that one be?

It was early morning by this time, and five-thirty was coming fast. I was totally unaware that my sister Jill had been awakened by God at five-thirty that morning. She had been reading the Psalms daily and just happened to be at chapters 118 and 119. As she began to read, she kept coming across scriptures about living and not dying. That's when God impressed on her heart that she needed to pray each of these prayers, just as if I was praying them. She began to declare the Word of God over my life and began praying "prayers of life, and not death," over me. That morning's prayers had started with Psalm 118:17, "I shall not die, but live, and declare the works of the Lord."

With more and more questions flooding my mind, I couldn't help but wonder how everything was going to transpire. Were they going to come in and give me a life-ending medication through my IV, or would they shoot me like they did the administrative attendant? My mind would not allow me to get any sleep. I couldn't help but wonder how the death would take place and how the family would react to the news. This seemed to drag on mercilessly through the early hours of the morning. I hadn't slept a wink.

Five-thirty finally came, and I was still alive. Why did they let me live? Did someone botch part of the plan? Did they just delay the time for an hour or so? What was going on? I was very worried about Melody and how she was handling all of this. Melody and I have been inseparable since I retired; we, normally, spent most of our time together, so to be apart was difficult for both of us.

A new nurse had come in after the morning shift change. I thought maybe she was unaware of what was happening, so I asked her if she could get my cell phone for me. It was in my bag containing clothing and other items that were brought into the hospital. I could see the bag from where I was lying in bed, but I didn't have the strength to get up, and I was hooked up to the IV and oxygen and couldn't reach that far. I was shocked and disappointed when she refused, saying that she had other things that she had to do.

Now, I was finally convinced that word had been passed down, and they were keeping me from contacting my family to alert them. I needed to let my family know I was still alive and that I had not died during the night. I assumed from the conversations and the phone calls I'd heard that most of them probably thought that I was dead.

By now, it was after 8:00 a.m., and I didn't know what to do. I was totally helpless. Melody was sure to be panic-stricken along with all the other members of my family. I had a sister in New Mexico that couldn't reach me and wouldn't be able to come to the hospital; a brother and sister-in-law living in southern Washington, who had been at my bedside just days prior; and a sister that lived in Colorado. My son and daughter both lived in Oregon and had been with me at the onset of this ordeal and gone home. I couldn't contact any of them, and I didn't know what to do.

The time slipped by slowly, eight-thirty, nine o'clock, nine-thirty all came and went, and still no communication with the family. I was devastated by this time. I was becoming frantic; every nerve in my body was on edge. Then, the most distraught time of my life was ripped open in a second, by the greatest elation ever.

At nine forty-five, Melody walked through the door of my room.

CHAPTER 1

The Backstory

It was a rainy day that Thursday afternoon on February 19, 1959, as were so many days during the winter and early spring, in Bremerton, Washington. It had been the typical kind of day, going to school and working on the assignments that my third-grade teacher, Mrs. Kock, had given all her students to complete at home.

After completing my homework, it was normal for me to go outside and play football, or some other type of sport, with David Harris, Kenneth Stansberry, my brother, and other friends of mine. But Thursdays, we had the Good News Club at my house. I had expected to see everyone beginning to arrive, like they did every Thursday after school. But for some unknown reason, today was different. Normally, the kids in the neighborhood would be trickling in by now.

The delicious aroma of my mom's freshly baked cookies and the jubilant sound of excitement, as all the kids would be arriving, were not only typical, but anticipated, every Thursday afternoon. But this particular day, they weren't there. The house was empty except for my mom and older sister, and they were crying. What was so terrible that would have caused them to be in tears? And why weren't we having the Good News Club?

I could only think the worst. Did my baby sister, who was a little over one and half years old, die or get very, very sick? I had walked home from school with my brother, so I knew he was okay.

Mom had finally stopped crying and wiped away her sniffles, long enough, to explain. My dad had been in an accident on his way home from an appointment in Tacoma, Washington. He worked as a sales representative for a major jewelry company and had traveled the thirty-six mile journey to his first appointment. As he was driving, he could see in the near distance a vehicle passing another car, traveling in the opposite direction. The driver couldn't get back on his side of the road in time, and the vehicle slammed into the 1951 black Chrysler New Yorker that my dad was driving. My dad swerved to get off the road, doing everything he could to get out of the way, but the oncoming vehicle hit his car broadside and pushed the Chrysler down an embankment. It was bad enough, seeing the shattered glass and hearing the horrific sound of metal being wrinkled up like a discarded piece of paper. But now, my dad's left knee had been forced up underneath the dashboard, leaving him, seemingly, trapped in his car. There were no seat belts back in those days, so he'd experienced a lot of jostling around during the calamity.

The police were called, and an ambulance arrived on the scene shortly after the vehicles had come to an abrupt stop. After assessing my dad's injuries, it was determined that he needed to go to the hospital. The team from the ambulance worked quickly and diligently to free his knee from the mangled dashboard and loaded him into the ambulance.

When my mom had finished telling me and my brother the story of what had happened to my dad, I felt relieved that my baby sister was okay. But now, in my little nine-year-old mind, I was trying to figure out what my dad was going to do. Was he going to be okay? Would he ever come home again? I wanted to cry, but I felt like I needed to be strong for my mom and my older sister, who were both still crying.

My dad's injuries were severe enough that he had been admitted into the hospital. But after just a few days, he was released to come home. Even though his stay in the hospital was short, he still had a long road ahead of him while he healed from the injuries.

As a result of the collision, my dad was laid up for an extended period of time. The jewelry company he had been working for, when he got into the accident, had no other choice but to sever their employment relationship with him.

During Dad's time at home, he spent much time in prayer and seeking the will of the Lord as to what his future was going to be.

At this time, he began to feel that he was supposed to use a gift and talent which he had discovered early on in his life. At the age of sixteen, a businessman had moved next to their family farm in North Dakota. This business man was also a pilot and owned a plane. That's when my dad took an interest in flying. The family became acquainted with their new neighbor, the businessman/pilot, fairly quickly. It wasn't long before he offered to give this young man, my dad, flying lessons, just as long as *his* father approved. After obtaining permission, my dad began taking lessons.

Time passed quickly, and on December 7, 1941, the radio blared, "Japs bomb Pearl Harbor." Dad was only twenty years old, but he had convinced his father that he needed to join with the other young men and serve our country. He needed written permission, and once his father was sure that my dad fully understood what this commitment meant, he agreed to sign yet another consent form. That signed paper allowed him to join the US Army Air Corps, where he was assigned to a squadron of A-24 dive bombers. He spent three and one-half years in the South Pacific.

While healing and having all this time to ponder and pray about what his future would hold, my dad could only wonder what the Lord had for him, following the life-changing car crash. Both my mom and dad had taken advantage of the time together, to talk and pray, and seek the Lord's will for our family.

One day, after much prayer, they decided to pick up roots in Bremerton, Washington, and move the family to Papua, New Guinea, where my dad could use his piloting experience. This new opportunity would allow him to fly missionaries and supplies into the jungle to support the work going on in those remote areas. This new plan felt right as my dad had been stationed in New Guinea while in the Army Corps and felt a drawing to go back again. The pieces seemed to be coming together quickly, and what a perfect fit!

The first step he would need to take would be to apply. So after contacting Missionary Aviation Fellowship, in southern California, and applying for a position as a pilot with the mission board, our family packed all our belongings, put them in crates, and sent them to San Diego, California, where my uncle lived. We were now on our way to Fullerton, California, the home of Mission Aviation Fellowship.

We had learned, during the application process, that it would be a couple weeks before we would know whether or not my dad's application would be accepted. So he and mom decided to take the family, and travel to San Diego, where we would spend some time with my uncle Bill and aunt Judy, while waiting for an answer.

We had such a great time with our family and immensely enjoyed the warmth of southern California and all the interesting sights. The warm sunny days, the California beaches, and the lifestyle were all a welcomed change from the cold and rainy days we were used to in the northwest. And after everything we had just been through, this was a time of refreshing for us, possibly a new beginning. We had hope that life was going to change for the good.

It seemed like it had been a long time since my dad had applied for the position with Missionary Aviation Fellowship. Although we, kids, had been having so much fun, the time went by pretty quickly. We all waited with excitement and anticipation as Dad finally received word from the mission board.

The day we'd been waiting for had arrived! Unfortunately, it was not what he had expected and, to say the least, a bit disappointing. Missionary Aviation Fellowship had rejected my dad's application. The reason for being rejected was that the cut-off age for the position he was seeking to attain was thirty-six, and he was thirty-eight, therefore, disqualifying him.

Mom and Dad's journey of faith was only beginning. This is when God begins to prove a person's faith; no job, no house, no income of any kind, and after stepping out in faith to enter God's mission field, it all seemed to be unraveling, and quickly. Would they continue to trust God and keep moving forward, seeking Him and His will? Or would they go back to where they started, feeling defeated and abandoned by God? This was a new place of trust. They thought they had been obedient to a call, only to find out that door was shut tight and never to be opened again. Where would they go from here? Dad had been tested before and *knew* that God would not let him down, even though the circumstances were trying to convince him differently. He had always hung on to God's promises. Since his car accident, he had become well-acquainted with Hebrews 13:5 that promised, "I will never leave thee, nor forsake thee," as well as Deuteronomy 31:8, where again, He promised, "The Lord himself goes before you and will be with you; he will never leave you nor forsake you. Do not be afraid; do not be discouraged."

Dad decided, that as a family, we would forge onward. He felt led to go to Albuquerque to visit with our great-grandma and spend a few days there. Great-grandma had a "special" relationship with God, where she would hear His voice audibly, and Dad had confidence in God and in great-grandma. He knew that she would not advise him according to her own counsel, but that she would only seek her Heavenly Father's counsel. And that's what he needed now, more than ever. He needed to know what God was saying and what our next step was going to be. He needed direction, divine direction. And he needed it fast!

While Dad was getting all the details for the sudden change in plans of heading to Albuquerque, Mom told us kids what we were going to do next and instructed us to get our things together and packed in our suitcases. Once again, we were all excited for what was ahead. We said our goodbyes to my aunt, uncle, and cousins in San Diego and were soon situated in our salmon-colored 1953 Imperial Chrysler, ready for the long trip to Albuquerque. Dad had purchased the Imperial when the '51 New Yorker had been totaled in the accident.

We were finally on the road and heading toward our next destination in New Mexico. On the way, Dad had prayed and asked the Lord to show us what He had for us as our next step. We knew about going to Great-grandma's house, but that was all. What we didn't realize was that, as children, we were learning the importance of continuing to trust in the Lord, even when things didn't look as we had envisioned or planned. As kids, we had no idea how these events would play out in our own lives of faith once *we* had entered into adulthood.

The trip was not only long but hot through the Arizona desert. The car was big, but even in that, there were six of us, and all our "stuff" was packed in there with us. In Flagstaff, we had driven into a horrific sandstorm and, along with the heat, made it very uncomfortable for the entire family. We weren't able to roll down the windows because the blowing sand would have filled the car. And we didn't have air conditioning, so it was hot and miserable. But we eventually drove out of the sandstorm, making the rest of the trip much more tolerable.

We had finally arrived in Albuquerque! It was such a joy to meet our great-grandma for the first time. She was eighty-three years old but full of spunk and very lively for her age. Mom had talked to us about our great-grandma having such a great sense of humor, but we never expected to her to be so funny and happy. She was fun to be around and a very gracious hostess. Her home was set up for entertaining, and she even had a pool table, just waiting for somebody to play. My brother, Bruce, and I quickly took advantage of that and spent time playing pool. When we got tired of doing that, we would go out in the backyard and throw around a ball to keep us busy.

Great-grandma said we could stay with her until the Lord revealed where we were to move. As she and my parents talked together, Dad explained to her exactly what had transpired: from where this venture had all started, when he thought we were supposed to go to the mission field; then the mission board rejected his application; to the present, wondering what the next step was going to be.

Great-grandma was a very godly woman, who knew how to reach the Throne Room of God. As soon as Dad was finished telling her all that had happened, she politely excused herself and immediately went into her bedroom to talk with her Heavenly Father. She had been gone for a while, and when she returned, she said that God had told her we were to go to Grants, New Mexico. Grants was about seventy-five miles northwest of Albuquerque.

So out of faith and trust in God, we all packed into the car once again and made the hour-and-a-half trip back to Grants. That night, we stayed in a motel room— Mom, Dad, and us, four kids—not making for very a cozy night for any of us.

The next morning, Dad was eager to get started looking for the job the Lord had in store for him. Mom and us, kids, spent the entire day in the motel room, while Dad went to several places, looking for employment. We waited patiently, anticipating the good news for what the Lord was going to provide. But as the day went on, it was getting later and later, and we hadn't heard from him. Finally, we heard the car drive up in front of the motel room. We were so excited to hear what God had done!

The look on Dad's face told it all. He got out of the car and came into the motel room to explain what had happened. The bottom line was, there were no open doors, and that meant he still didn't have a job. It was all so confusing. There were so many questions, and yet, no answers. At least not that we could see right now.

So we gathered as a family in that little motel room and did the only thing my dad knew to do: we prayed. What else do you do when God doesn't do things the way you expected Him to?

In the book of John, we find the story of Lazarus. He and his two sisters, Mary and Martha, had become very good friends with Jesus. They had spent a lot of time with Him in their home, eating together and learning about the kingdom of God. But one day, while Jesus had been traveling in a distant town, Lazarus became very sick and was nearing death. When Mary and Martha and all their close friends decided there was nothing more they could do, it was determined that Mary and Martha should go and find Jesus. They were going to let Him know how desperately and urgently they needed Him to come and heal Lazarus. They knew this was nothing short of a miracle, a miracle they were confident would only be possible with Jesus.

But as we find out, when we continue to read the story, instead of Jesus responding to their request and leaving immediately, He chose to wait for two more days. He even told Mary and Martha that the sickness was not unto death but for the glory of God, so that He, the Son of God, would be glorified through it.

When He did finally decide it was time to make the journey to where Lazarus was, He told His disciples that their friend was asleep, and He needed to go and wake him up. The disciples thought if Lazarus was just sleeping, then there would be no rush to get back because sleeping would help him heal. Jesus finally told them that

Lazarus was dead. Apparently, He knew something they didn't in the planning of all this.

Once Jesus arrived, he found that Lazarus had been pronounced dead and had already been in the tomb for four days. Of course, Martha and Mary were devastated! It almost seemed like Jesus didn't care. When they heard that Jesus was back in town, Martha even questioned Him as to why He had waited so long. She told Him, if He had been there sooner, Lazarus wouldn't have died!

Was Jesus late? Did He miss His timing? It would have looked that way. But God's ways and His timing are not always the same as ours. God may have a better plan that will increase our trust and belief in Him that wouldn't otherwise happen if He did everything the way we expected. Many times, He will choose to do things different so that we *know* it was *He* that did it, no question about it. And as we will discover in the chapters ahead, that's exactly how He was about to work again and again.

CHAPTER 2

God's Timing

Time was of the essence, as it always is, when we find ourselves in an uncontrollable situation, and we need answers quickly. Mary and Martha had personally communicated to Jesus how urgent it was that He immediately attended to their request, but Lazarus had died while they were waiting for Him. By the time Jesus had arrived at Mary and Martha's house, Lazarus had already been dead for four days.

Martha had to have been discouraged, disappointed, and disillusioned by this time. This was not how she thought it would go. She had her own idea of how she *thought* Jesus would handle things, but everything looked hopeless now. Only a miracle could fix this.

Martha's disappointment would play out as she went out to meet Jesus upon His arriving back into town. She was still trying to make sense of what happened when she cried out to Him, pleading, "Lord, if you had been here, my brother would not have died. But even now I know that whatever you ask from God, God will give you." Martha and Mary believed this with all their hearts. They had already witnessed many miracles, including healing, and Mary, herself, had experienced the casting out of seven demons. Nothing would be impossible for Jesus.

Jesus had a different plan. His plan was much bigger and was about to prove to all who were witnessing this event the reality of the Resurrection He had been teaching His disciples. He wanted them to understand the spiritual implications of it. Jesus was about to give conclusive proof that He truly was the Resurrection and the Life

(John 11:25) and that He was the Son of God and had the power of life and death.

Jesus knew all along what the plan for Lazarus was, but when He saw Mary and Martha weeping, He was troubled. When Jesus asked them where Lazarus's body had been laid, they quickly took Him to the tomb. Jesus told them to move the stone away from the tomb, and when they did, Jesus yelled out with a loud voice, "Lazarus, come forth!" He must have cried loud enough so that everyone there could hear His command and *know* they had just witnessed a miracle, without any doubt. There could be no doubt that Lazarus had surely died, and only God could have raised someone to life again.

God's ultimate plan had been accomplished! Jesus did *more* than just heal; He gave evidence to the fact that He was indeed the Resurrection and the Life. Lazarus was healed, but Jesus chose *the path* to his healing.

Our family was now in the same situation, *in need of a miracle*. Even though it was a different circumstance, it was the same lesson of learning to trust the *"ways" of God* and not our own. Great-grandma had clearly heard from God that we were supposed to move to Grants and that God had a job waiting there for my dad. But when my dad, in obedience, went there and knocked on all the doors, nothing opened. There was no job.

So after praying in that little motel room and asking God what we would should do, once again, Dad decided we needed to go back to Great-grandma's house in Albuquerque. When we drove up in her driveway, Great-grandma met us before we even got out of the car. She looked troubled, and we heard it in her voice when she asked, "What are you doing back here? God said you were to be in Grants!" She acted extremely surprised to see us back so soon.

Dad explained to her that he didn't have enough information yet as to what he was supposed to do in Grants and expressed his concern to Great-grandma. He hadn't been able to find a job, and we needed a place to live, not to mention we had run out of the financial means to secure a place to live. It all seemed so overwhelming to him.

She invited us to come into the house, and so we followed her inside. Great-grandma had such a close relationship with God and was convinced God had already given clear instructions the first time. She turned to Dad and said, "Let me go talk to the Lord and see if it's okay for you to spend the night here tonight." Once again, she entered her bedroom to meet with Father God to express her concerns and requests to Him. This time, He spoke to her in an audible voice. When she returned from speaking with Him, she said, "The Lord told me that it would be okay for you to stay here tonight, but tomorrow, you need to go back to Grants. He has a job for you there."

The next morning, after having breakfast, Great-grandma prayed for Dad and sent us on our way. We went back to Grants, just as God had instructed. The first place Dad applied, the door opened. It was a bookkeeper's position with Conly Motors. During the interview, the owner indicated that he wanted Dad to start the next day. When he hesitated, the owner inquired a bit further. Dad told him that we had just moved here and didn't have a place to live. The owner responded quickly, "That's not a problem. I own a rental that just came available. You and your family are welcome to rent it." Again, Dad hesitated in his response, and again, the owner realized something wasn't right. So, he asked, "Is there something wrong?"

Dad, feeling a little embarrassed, answered, "We've had some hard times just getting to this point, and we've exhausted our finances. There's no way that I can come up with the rent and deposit for the house. Don't get me wrong, I would love the opportunity to do all of this, the job and the house, but I just don't see how that would be possible with our current financial situation."

At that moment, a miracle happened. The owners' heart was turned with compassion toward my dad and our circumstances. Dad watched as the owner of Conly Motors picked up a pen and started scratching out some numbers on his little notepad. Within just a few short minutes, he had worked out a financial plan with my dad so we could move into the house immediately. The owner of the business had just provided everything we needed to get established in Grants, New Mexico.

Top left to right: my Mom and Jackie; Bottom left to right: Jill, me, and Bruce

We never really know how God is working the circumstances in our lives to bring about His desired intentions for us, intentions to do us good. But our participation in faith is required for Him to complete the process. Persistence is a must in following the Lord and trusting Him every step of the way, will *never* fail. Sometimes it may look like it, but His testing requires that we not give up. Faith is a *must,* and the passing of God's test *will* result in our spiritual growth. This pleases Him very much! Hebrews 11:6 says, "And without faith it is impossible to please God."

Dad stayed at that bookkeeping position with Conly Motors for about three months before he was offered a job with James Hamilton Construction in Milan, New Mexico, where he would receive a substantial raise in pay. Again, he would be the bookkeeper for Mr. Hamilton. It was at this time we found a church home, and Grace Baptist Church became a launching pad for spiritual growth in brand new ways.

We loved our new church and began making friends with other attendees very quickly. One of the families that we met early on was the Leon Friend family. They were missionaries to the Navajo's. My dad loved missions and felt drawn to become a part of what they were doing. As he began to spend time with them, his love for the Navajo people grew. And once my dad began to learn about their culture, he realized even more how much they needed to know the truth of Jesus.

Our family had decided to move a little farther out from town so we could be closer to the Friend family. They lived in Thoreau, New Mexico, which placed us within twenty minutes of their home. The town was a part of the Navajo Indian Reservation and was the village where my dad and Leon would visit with the Navajo families.

My dad enjoyed meeting with the different families and, as time went on, began driving the old church bus out to the little village on Sundays. We would go to church in Grants in the morning, and in the afternoon, Dad would head back to Thoreau to get the bus. My older sister, Jackie, would usually go with him to pick up the children in the village and bring them to the little mission church. They loved singing and hearing stories about Jesus.

One Sunday, he took me with him rather than my oldest sister, Jackie. My dad drove the little bus, and I eagerly sat next to him, watching as we picked up both children and adults, each from their own little Hogan, so they could attend the church service that morning. It was a warm day, and it seemed like everyone was in a good mood, as the noise in the bus seemed louder than normal and it had a festive feel to it. When we arrived at the church, everyone piled out and hurriedly found their places to sit in the church building. The service was filled with singing where they clapped their hands and sang to the Lord. It had been such a good day. Everyone was so happy as they climbed back into the bus for the thirty-minute ride back home.

On the way back to their homes, my dad called for me to come to the front of the bus where I could sit close to him. We were already back in the village and driving on the dirt roads. We went from Hogan to Hogan, letting the children and adults off the bus so they could go home. As we were nearing one Hogan, my dad leaned over, and in a whisper, he asked me, "Do you see that woman?"

I looked out the window and saw an older woman, probably in her seventies or eighties. She was staring at Dad with a glare in her eyes that was very hateful and with an expression of anger on her face. I answered, "Yah, who is she?"

He responded, "She's the mother and grandmother to the family that just got off the bus, and she hates me."

I couldn't understand why she would hate my dad. My dad loved everybody on that bus and in that village. So I asked him, "Why does she hate you so much, Dad?" I was a little saddened by what my dad had just said.

He responded ever so quietly, and I thought he was going to cry. "She hates me because I love Jesus, and I want her family to know Jesus too. She's very mad at me for taking her family to church."

I was still a bit confused because I couldn't imagine anyone being mad about their family wanting to love Jesus. But as time went on, and I became more familiar with the ways of this older Navajo lady, I found out that she operated in witchcraft. I learned a few things about their beliefs and how everything seemed to be tied to a mysticism, including the types of homes they lived in.

Their Hogan was designed with a spiritual meaning behind it because of the beliefs of the Navajo's. My dad told me that the roof and sides are all rounded to keep evil spirits from hiding in the corners. The fire was placed on the hard-packed floor beneath the smoke hole and a flap or hinged door covered the doorway. Traditionally, the Hogan didn't have any windows and was only ventilated by the smoke hole in the roof and the east-facing doorway.

The Hogan was more than just a place to eat and sleep and the concept of it as a "home" bore little resemblance to the kind of home we lived in. The Hogan was considered a gift of the gods, and as such, it occupied a place in the sacred world. The round Hogan was symbolic of the sun, and its door faced east so that the first thing that a Navajo family saw in the morning was the rising sun . . . Father Sun, one of the most revered deities of the Navajo. The construction of a new Hogan was almost always a community affair. Once completed, the new Hogan was consecrated with a Blessing Way rite whereby the Holy People were asked to "let this place be happy."

That God-ordained encounter with the Navajo woman would change the rest of my life in ways beyond what I could have ever imagined. And the understanding of it wouldn't come until many, many years later.

That specific incident made a profound impact on my life in a most dramatic way. I didn't know anything had happened at that time, but as I look back on my life, it affected me dramatically and throughout my life as God has granted me His favor and protection.

It's interesting how we see every event as just an event, without ever realizing how God has woven together each circumstance to form a perfect picture in His ultimate plan for our life. My sister, Jill Cromwell, wrote a book called *The Tapestry God's Masterpiece*. If you've ever wondered the whys of the circumstances in your life and what God was doing, I recommend you read her book. Through her stories, life lessons, and journey with the Master Artist, she shares her own struggles and victories, teaching how God was weaving every detail of every circumstance she encountered, to form what she refers to as the tapestry of her life.

If you look at the back of a hand-crafted woven rug, it looks like a mess without direction or purpose. But if you turn it over, it is a beautiful sculpture that has been carefully and methodically created by a master artist's hand. That's how God works in our lives. We may not see the beauty that is taking place on the back side of the tapestry of our life, but God is weaving each and every event and circumstance that happens to us good or seemingly bad. He has a perfect and beautiful plan for us. It's the Master's plan.

Throughout Scripture, we can see how different individuals had to go through extreme circumstances, which allowed God the opportunity to perform miracles and bestow His blessings.

For example, remember the story of Job and what terrible things happened to him? But in the end, he became more prosperous and fruitful than he was in the beginning. In Job 42:10, it states, "After Job had prayed for his friends, the Lord restored his fortunes and gave him twice as much as he had before."

Another example is the story of Joseph, who was shunned by his family. They even wanted to kill him, but God saved his life. After being falsely accused, thrown into prison, and then elevated to a very high position in Egypt, he was able, through God's direction and plan, to prepare and store enough food in advance of a seven-year famine in Egypt. This was to fulfill God's purpose in Joseph's life and fulfill the promise He had given Joseph through a dream he'd had when he was just a child. Joseph not only provided enough food for all of Egypt, but this supply would lead to the feeding of his own family. In the end, he told his brothers, "You intended to harm me, but God intended it for good to accomplish what is now being done, the saving of many lives" (Gen. 50:20).

As you continue to read the stories in the up-coming chapters, the circumstances in my life may appear to look very negative. How could a loving God allow such things to happen to His child? What good could ever come from it? But be encouraged, God knows what He's doing. He sees the big picture.

CHAPTER 3

Working for Our Good

Many of us have been through events and circumstance in our own lives that, as we look back, had the potential to bring death. Those times are very vivid in our memories, and then we realize it was only by the grace of God that our lives were saved.

In John 16:33 (KJV), Jesus said, "In this world ye shall have tribulation." The New International Version says it this way, "In this world you will have trouble." I doubt that any of us would disagree with that statement. The Greek word for tribulation or trouble in that verse is the word *thlipsis*, which means anguish, burden, or persecution. And it's something we have all faced in one way or another. We've all had our share of experiences that have brought trouble.

Leonardo DiCaprio tells of a time when a great white shark jumped into his cage when he was diving in South Africa. The actor said, "Half of the shark's body was in the cage, and it was snapping at me. Surprised and perplexed, I fell to the bottom of the cage and tried to lie flat. The great white took about five or six snaps, an arm's length away from my head. Then it flipped itself back out of the cage. The guys there said that had never happened in the thirty years they'd been doing this."

You may have read the story of Colton Burpo. He was the four-year-old son of a small-town Nebraska pastor, who slipped from consciousness during emergency surgery and claimed to have entered heaven. He survived and later began talking about his experience. He remembered looking down and seeing the doctor operating on him but also was also able to see his dad praying in the waiting room.

The family didn't know what to believe, but the evidence would become clear as Colton began to tell stories of events he had no way of knowing. Colton said he met his sister while he was in heaven and had even been told her name. His mom had miscarried a baby girl several years earlier but hadn't told Colton. Then he met his great-grandfather who had died thirty years before Colton was born. Colton shared impossible-to-know details about each incident that happened between his dad and his great-grandfather.

Near-death experiences are definitely real and seem to be somewhat common. And if you search them out, each one is unique in its own way. Some people give God the glory for their experience, while others seem to just chalk theirs up to "luck." Just walk into a bookstore and you'll find book after book filled with the experience of someone dying and coming back to life again. There are thousands upon thousands of testimonials.

In 2 Timothy 3:12, Paul writes, "Everyone who wants to live a Godly life in Christ Jesus *will be* persecuted." As a matter of fact, we all will face things throughout our lives that will be unpleasant or even painful in one way or another. Anguish, burden, persecution, we've all experienced at least one of them at some time in our lives. It may have been from a bad choice and, therefore, becomes a consequence of our own carelessness. But there are times when the sufferings we encounter may be from a spiritual force that wants to disrupt or end our God-intended purpose in life.

One of those encounters happened to me after I graduated from high school. In 1968, as my senior year was coming to an end, our country was heavily involved in the Vietnam War. Most of the young men, eighteen years of age or older, were being drafted into one of the military branches: Army, Navy, Marines, or Air Force. Many of these young men were being shipped out to fight in that war.

One day during the school year, Steve Seely, a friend of mine, and I decided instead of waiting to be drafted because many of the draftees were being sent to Nam, we would *voluntarily* join the Navy.

We were promised we could choose where we wanted to go and that the two of us would be able to stay together for the remainder of our three-year active duty enlistment. As it turned out, we didn't even go to boot camp together. I did my boot camp training at the Naval Air Base in Sandpoint, Washington, and Steve was sent to Millinton, Tennessee, just outside Memphis. And we *didn't* get assigned to the same unit as promised. As a matter of fact, I received orders to the Naval Air Station in Bloomington, Minnesota, just outside Minneapolis. And we never had a time when we were together throughout our years in the military. We felt like we had been tricked.

When I had first arrived at the Naval Air Station in Minnesota, I would go to the end of the runway at night and look up to the blackened sky. Through the darkness, thousands of twinkling stars lit up the dark sky above me. I felt such a sense of awe for my Creator, and my heart was filled with so much gratitude toward Him. As I lifted my head and my hands toward the heavens, I lifted my voice to God and reminded Him that I would give Him everything. I really did mean what I was saying, but I always had a condition in my heart. I added, *"If you will let me go home."*

Prior to going on active duty, I was a Weekend Warrior, meaning I went to a weekend meeting once a month to learn and practice what we would need to know before going on active duty, or at least, be ready in case they needed more enlisted men to be activated if the war escalated.

One cold, snowy, and icy Sunday morning as I woke up, it felt like just another normal day. However, this was the weekend I was supposed to attend the regularly scheduled monthly meeting for the Weekend Warriors. So after lying in bed and soaking in as much rest as I could, it was inevitable that I was going to have to get up and get going. I leisurely fixed a pot of coffee and ate some breakfast, then got dressed into my Navy uniform, which was required when attending these meetings. I started my old 1964 Volkswagen bug and quickly turned the heater on high, while I brushed the snow from its hood and fenders and scraped the ice off the windows. It felt extremely cold, and I was hoping to get a head start on the heater. I left the house and began driving my usual route, heading toward the freeway. My little car had finally started warming up, and I was just beginning to get comfortable. As I started to head on to the freeway entrance, I accelerated due to the lack of power in the VW, so I could easily merge into the flow of traffic. I had no idea how icy the roads were, when suddenly, I hit a patch of black ice. I began spinning and ended up going backward across the snowy grass median and into the on-coming traffic.

Everything was moving in slow motion. I was downshifting because I knew if I hit the brakes, I'd really be in trouble. When I looked out the side window, there was traffic headed my way. The first vehicle I spotted was a two-tank gas truck. I was sliding; he was sliding; and smash! He ran over my engine. The engine of my car was literally touching the pavement.

The truck driver had moved his truck to the far right-hand side of the road, while at that same moment, my car started spinning around. When the spinning motion began to slow down, I looked and saw another car heading right toward me. Again, this guy was slipping and sliding all over the place and ran into the back of my car. This went on as four other cars, all out of control, did the same thing. I felt like I was inside a pinball machine, and everyone was taking pot-shots at me.

By the time it was over, I was sitting in the middle of the freeway, traffic was stopped for a long way back, and I was trying to wrap my head around everything that had just taken place. I got out of my little jalopy, and everybody came running over to see if I was okay. It was a bit hectic, as there were several smashed vehicles, stopped in the middle of the freeway. It wasn't long before the police and tow trucks showed up on the scene, and after determining there were no serious injuries, the tow truck drivers began to load up all the damaged vehicles. The driver who was taking my car told me to get in, and he would take me to the shop where my car would be fixed.

Now I had to call my dad. This was the part I dreaded from the beginning of the mishap. The only thing I could think of was that he was going to be really mad since I was listed on his insurance policy, and now his insurance was going to go up.

When we finally arrived at the repair shop, I had worked through most of what had happened and what I was going to need to do now that I didn't have a car. I realized that everything was going to be all right when I called my dad. But as I thought about everything that *could* have happened to me, I began to realize how close I was to having been seriously hurt, or worse yet, I could have been killed.

It was like a miracle! I had only bumped my head on the windshield. Back in 1968, cars didn't have seat belts, at least the cars I could afford. A two-tank gas truck and five other vehicles had hit me. And the only injury, which wasn't really an injury at all, was a bump on the head. I knew this had to be God's providential protection over me.

That night I went to church. During the service, they had a time where people could stand and give a testimony of something that God had done in their lives. I knew I had to stand up and tell the story of what had happened to me that morning. I told the congregation of my experience and that God had spared my life for a reason. As I spoke, I began to realize so many things about my life, about God, and what He might have planned for me. That accident got my attention. I prayed and told God that I would do *anything* He wanted me to do. That night, I surrendered my life completely to God, and I was serious. He really could have all my life to do as He pleased.

By the way, God doesn't play games. If you surrender your life to Him, He takes you seriously. Sometimes, our promises to Him are really for our advantage. We are not truly ready to sacrifice in the way He wants us to sacrifice. So many times, we *think* our motives are pure in offering our lives to Him, but when our hearts are tested, we find that there were hidden agendas or conditions that we expected to be met. Unfortunately, that was the condition of my heart before the accident. I was willing to give God everything *if* He met my condition of letting me go back home to Seattle. I didn't know it then, but there were many lessons I needed to learn along life's pathway. And I had no idea that I would mess up, over and over again, while trying to learn those lessons.

But what if we do fail the lesson? When entertaining that question, my mind is turned to a familiar passage in the Bible, and how the picture that Jesus gave represents God's attitude when a child of God messes up.

Number one, He will *allow* us to mess up even if it's not what He desires from us. God created us with a free will, and He will not *make* us do anything. We all have choices.

Number two, there will be consequences for our actions. We cannot blame God for the results of our own choices. A quote from an unknown author, says

> You call Me Eternal, then do not seek Me.
> You call Me Fair, then do not love Me.
> You call Me Gracious, then do not trust Me.
> You call Me Just, then do not fear Me.
> You call Me Life, then do not choose Me.
> You call Me Light, then do not see Me.
> You call Me Lord, then do not respect Me.
> You call Me Master, then do not obey Me.
> You call Me Merciful, then do not thank Me.
> You call Me Mighty, then do not honor Me.
> You call Me Noble, then do not serve Me.
> You call Me Rich, then do not ask Me.
> You call Me Savior, then do not praise Me.
> You call Me Shepherd, then do not follow Me.
> You call Me the Way, then do not walk with Me.
> You call Me Wise, then do not heed Me.
> You call Me Son of God, then do not worship Me.
> When I discipline you, then do not blame Me.

And number three, He will meet you with open arms when you return. The familiar passage that I am referring to is recorded in Luke 15:11–32. It is commonly known as the parable of the Prodigal Son.

The story of the Prodigal Son demonstrates how our Heavenly Father runs to us when we come to Him with a repentant heart after running the course of doing things our way. It begins with a man who has two sons. The younger son asked his father for his portion of the family estate as an early inheritance. His dad allowed it, and immediately, the son received his portion. Right away, he decided to go on a long journey to a distant land and began squandering away his fortune on wild living.

Time passed, and when the money ran out, a severe famine hit the country, and the son found himself in dire circumstances. He took a job feeding pigs. Eventually, he became bankrupt, so dead broke that he even wished to eat the food given to the pigs.

When this young man finally came to his senses, he began to think about his father. In humility, he recognized his foolishness and decided to return to his father and ask for forgiveness and mercy.

The father who represents Father God in this parable had been watching and waiting for the time his son would return home again. As soon as his father saw his son, he received his son back with open arms of compassion. He was overjoyed by the return of his lost son. As a matter of fact, as soon as they embraced, the father ordered an enormous feast in celebration of his son's return.

The picture is so clear! God allows us to mess up, then He waits for us to return. For some of us, it's longer than others, but He always welcomes us back with open arms when we *do* come back home to Him.

Throughout my life, I have seen how God has protected me from danger and near-disasters. But then, there have been those times when He allowed me to go through things to draw me closer to Him. These lessons were intended for the purpose of waking me up to the fact that I was headed in the wrong direction, or to slow me down long enough so that I would listen to Him.

God, in all His lovingkindness and with tender mercies, showed me grace and brought me closer to Him through the near-fatal accident that Sunday morning. But there was even more to that than just saving my life from death. He showed me how serious He was about my relationship with Him. How far will He go to prove to us how much He loves us and desires our hearts? I can tell you from my own experience that He will go however far it takes. He loves us *that much*!

CHAPTER 4

The Journey Begins

Over forty years had passed since my accident. God had taught me so many lessons, some easier than others, but through them all, my relationship with the Lord had grown immensely. I learned to trust Him and follow Him no matter what the circumstances looked like. However, the next lessons He had to teach me would be more than anything I could have ever imagined. There would be new lessons taught in a new manner that would take me into a deeper relationship with the Lord than I had ever experienced.

It was 2008, Thanksgiving weekend. Melody, my wife, and I had planned to spend the weekend relaxing since we had four days off together. She was a teacher at a child daycare center in downtown Seattle. Her job was both strenuous physically and stressful mentally and emotionally. I was a district sales manager in Bellevue and was also feeling the strain of working too many hours, along with the pressures of meeting quotas. We were both looking forward to the much-needed rest.

We relaxed on Thursday, enjoying Thanksgiving by going to a restaurant and having a pleasant lunch. Then we were able to enjoy a great afternoon of tranquility, which was a much-welcomed leisure.

On Friday, Melody had to do some grocery shopping, and I decided to do a little house cleaning while she was gone. The normal chores of vacuuming, dusting, and mopping went smoothly, until it came to cleaning the bathtub. My usual kneeling beside the tub was replaced by removing my shoes and socks and climbing into the tub, with the intent of deep scrubbing and then rinsing with the shower attachment.

As I bent over, a very sharp, excruciating pain pierced my back. My knees buckled, and I ended up kneeling on the tub floor. The pain wasn't foreign to me as I had experienced the exact severe ache previously, beginning in my back and working through to my stomach. I'd had kidney stones two other times that felt exactly like this pain. My first thought was to go to the emergency room as I had done in the past. But remembering how they dealt with the stones, I decided to immolate what they did and just hydrate and let nature take care of the rest. I would then wait until the stones were released from my body.

I began drinking a lot of water and nature began to take its course, but no stones appeared, and the searing pain continued. Melody had just returned from shopping, and I told her what had happened. She immediately suggested I go to the emergency room and drove me to Swedish Medical Center in Seattle, which was only a ten-minute drive from our home.

Upon arrival, I was checked in and they took some X-rays, then I was given a room where we were supposed to wait for the results. After the expected delay, the doctor came in with the diagnosis. Much to our surprise, there were no kidney stones. Instead, they needed to perform more tests and planned to take a biopsy of my lymph nodes. I was told it would take about three days to get the results back, and I should call and get their findings.

Following a simple procedure where they cut a small incision into my groin area, I then got dressed, and Melody and I went home. The pain was still there, but at least it was bearable, not as extreme as I had experienced before, while we waited for answers. As Melody and I talked, we were both somewhat disturbed by the idea of it possibly being cancer, so we prayed and waited.

Both of us continued with our regular work schedules, and after three days, I called the hospital to get the results of my biopsies. It was a strange conversation, as they told me they didn't have any results for me, and that I needed to call back in another three days. This just added to the uneasy feeling we already had regarding a possible case of cancer.

Another three days passed, and I called the hospital again. This time, when they asked my name, there was a short pause, then the nurse came back on the line and asked for my social security number. I gave it to her, and she put me on hold again. I began feeling a little irritated as I had to wait when I had anticipated getting a quick answer. After waiting a couple of minutes, the lady came back on the line and asked for my address. Now, I was really starting to get mad. Another wait. The next and last time she took me off hold, the attendant informed me they couldn't find me in their system.

What?! A hospital that had taken X-rays, a biopsy, all my information, and they couldn't find me in their system? By this time, Melody was frantic. She demanded I go to another hospital and suggested using Virginia Mason, the same one where her dad had been. We immediately drove the few, short miles to that hospital and checked in to the emergency room, where we were able to explain what we had just encountered at the first hospital.

The nurses were a bit surprised by what they were hearing, especially with the sensitive nature as to what we were dealing with. Within a very short time, I went through the exact, same process as I'd gone through at the other hospital: X-ray, biopsy, and then another three-day wait.

When I called three days later, I was given the news we didn't want to hear. I had been diagnosed with non-Hodgkin lymphoma. This type of cancer starts in the white blood cells called *lymphocytes*, which are part of the body's immune system. Lymph nodes are bean-sized collections of lymphocytes, along with other immune system cells. They are all connected throughout the body, including inside the chest, abdomen, and pelvis. I was told that cancer starts when cells in the body begin to grow out of control. Cells in nearly any part of the body can become cancerous and can spread to other areas of the body. None of this was good news by any means. One of the nurses I spoke with said that lymphoma was the one type of cancer she feared most. That was something I definitely did not want to hear.

We had an appointment with the oncologist, and he explained what we needed, as well as some ideas and suggestions that would be helpful as we entered the chemotherapy treatments. We were given the option of going through a new experimental treatment or the treatment that was being done at that time. Melody and I chose the latter as we didn't have much knowledge on how chemotherapy affected patients.

The doctor advised us on the pros and cons of the treatment. Based on the information we were given, we decided to go with the twelve-week session. My regiment for treatment would require that I go in to the hospital as an out-patient for a chemotherapy treatment once every three weeks, receiving a total of four treatments over that twelve-week period. We were told by the oncologist that when the treatments were done, it would take another nine months to recover. Our idea was to get it done and over with and get back to living life as we were accustomed to.

There was a lot to process after talking with the oncologist. I knew that it was going to take a toll on my body and slow me down considerably. Both Melody and I were very aware that this was going to change our lifestyle tremendously, but since we'd never experienced anything like this before, we weren't quite sure what to expect. We drove home and began to pray for a complete healing. As we contacted each of our family members, they began to agree with us in prayer.

I knew that the side effects of the chemotherapy treatments had the potential to disrupt my ability to perform my job. So with that knowledge, I decided I needed to discuss my options with upper management where I worked. The next day, I went to the regional supervisor's office, sat down, and told him he would need to replace me as the district sales manager. He knew something hadn't been right and was glad I had made the effort to try and find a solution. We went to lunch together so I could explain in more detail everything that had taken place and the events that were about to take place. He was very understanding, and we discussed who would be the best replacement for me. The perfect person was agreed upon, and he began the process of making it happen. I stepped down from the district sales manager to a sales position since I had been informed by the oncologist that I wouldn't have the energy to continue at the pace I was going.

The next day, I began working as a sales person: calling, setting up appointments and then going out on the appointments, making presentations with the goal of selling the business on our service as a credit card processor. I was soon to realize that this was going to take much more energy than I had anticipated. I had started my regiment of chemotherapy treatments and quickly recognized that my job wasn't nearly as easy as it had been when I was healthy. I had only enough energy to work until two or two-thirty every day, and then I would have to go home and rest.

There were some days I would have to call in to work and let them know I needed to stay home as I was too sick to even get out of bed. My regional supervisor had been made aware that this would probably be the norm when I started the new position. And as the treatments continued, my energy level was continuing to spiral downward. I tried to keep the pace for the demands at work, but each day when I got home, I would go to bed.

It wasn't long after this that I entered a depression and didn't want to be around anyone. I was miserable. Melody would go to the video store and buy movies that I could watch to help take my mind off the gloomy cloud over my head. She was truly a godsend as she tried to make life a little brighter for me. I just wasn't happy, and I wasn't making anyone else happy either.

Depression is a very debilitating disorder that affects a large number of people worldwide. It can be difficult to work, study, sleep, eat, and enjoy activities with friends and family. It can also cause one to desire excessive sleep every day. There is sometimes a loss of interest in normal activities and relationships. I was experiencing all of these to some degree, and it was affecting my family relationships as well as my work-related performance.

At the time, I felt like life was never going to get better. There were so many ups and downs as I had begun the healing process. In the beginning, it seemed like I experienced way more downs than ups. I had never experienced depression, chemotherapy, or for that matter, sickness of any kind. I had always been healthy and, for the most part, very positive in my attitude. I had lots of goals, and with that, I had the energy and motivation to carry them out. Life had been good.

For over forty years since the accident, I had given my life wholly to the Lord and had experienced so many good things, never anticipating that I would live life any differently. I had trials and some difficult obstacles to overcome, but nothing that took me down. I knew how to overcome in the strength of the Lord, and I did. It was just the way I experienced God.

But now, things had changed, suddenly and drastically. God obviously had a different plan, and my path was going to get even rockier. My journey with cancer was only beginning, and I had no idea at that time in my life what would transpire next. God doesn't tell us what our future holds; He just assures us that He holds our future. He is the one leading us to our destiny according to His will, His plan, and His purpose. It is our responsibility to trust Him and follow. It's called faith.

CHAPTER 5

A Miraculous Provision

As the months passed, my body was still reacting to the effects of the chemotherapy treatments. The demands of my job on my mind and body were too much for me to keep up with. I was unable to keep the pace, which eventually led to losing my job.

Since I had no income coming in, I knew I had to do something, so I ended up going to the unemployment office to apply for benefits. I found the office closest to where we lived, filled out the required paperwork, and was told that I would need to speak to an unemployment representative.

At that same time, I was having a little difficulty hearing everything that people would say to me during a conversation. I waited my turn, and a young man came out and called my name. I followed him back to a small cubicle, and he began to ask me questions. After a short time of answering his questions, he asked me if I was hard of hearing. I was probably asking him to repeat himself more often than usual. I told him that it had been getting more difficult to make out what people were saying. Immediately, he asked if I had spent time in the military. I affirmed his observation with a *yes*. He then asked if I had ever reported the loss of hearing to the Department of Veterans Affairs. My answer to him was, "No, I had never even thought of it."

As the interview continued, he questioned me as to which branch of the service I served. I told him the Navy, and he continued the line of questioning with, "What did you do?"

I replied, "I was a storekeeper."

I'm not sure why he asked the next question. "Were you ever around airplanes?"

My reply was, "Yes, I spent quite a bit of time out on the flight line, delivering parts to the mechanics."

He then told me that I should at least go in and have a hearing test, that maybe my hearing loss was due to being around the loud noise of the jets. He had been so thorough with his questions, and it caught me off guard. I had heard so many horror stories of other veteran's experiences with the VA and wasn't sure if it would even be worth my time to pursue it.

In spite of my doubts, I followed that unemployment officer's advice and scheduled a hearing test. I called and set up an appointment at the local VA Health Care System in the Audio Clinic. I had never had a hearing test and was in store for a new experience. When I arrived for the appointment, I was given a packet of paperwork filled with questions to complete before they would even schedule an appointment.

The information they were seeking was quite extensive, to say the least. It required personal patient information, medical history, social history, health history, and many more questions. Upon completing the questionnaire, I was finally given a time and date for the hearing test.

The day arrived quickly for my appointment, and sure enough, it was an unusual experience. Listening and responding to what I heard in different formats, while all my responses were being recorded. I assumed they had to be sure there was permanent hearing loss, hence, the reason for such an extensive hearing test.

Now, all I needed to do was wait for their conclusion. I still wasn't convinced that anything would come of the whole procedure I had just gone through. But for some reason, I felt compelled to keep moving forward. At least, until the door closed. During the waiting period, I went home and resumed my normal activities.

The door never closed! In fact, they came back with good news. They had confirmed that I had inner ear damage and recommended that I apply for compensation. Once again, I filled out another lengthy application, and it was submitted to the proper authorities, who would determine as to whether or not I qualified for the compensation. And again, I found myself waiting for an answer. I was beginning to understand why veterans decided *not* to pursue VA benefits.

I'm so glad that I was persistent and didn't give up during the process. The results came back stating that I was approved and would receive monthly paychecks from the Veterans Administration. I was considered a disabled veteran, and that meant the VA would now pay for my medical bills including hospitalization. I had a small co-pay for medications, but otherwise, they would take care of me.

Nothing of what I had just achieved had any dramatic impact on me. At least, not right then. But God knew what was coming in the near future. He also knew what I was going to need. Everything that had just been accomplished would one day soon fall into place.

It was presently April 2013 and had been five years since Melody and I had first become aware of the cancer in my body. We had no idea, as I began chemotherapy, that the treatments would be the easy part in comparison to what I would experience during the recovery. And we were also unaware of the fact that the treatments would cause damage to my body, which would make the recovery process to be incredibly long and difficult.

At this point in time, I was dealing with serious weight loss along with problems urinating. I knew that with age, it's common to have to get up often in the night to use the bathroom, but the urgency had increased, and the weight loss had become a huge concern. My tendency, because of everything I had been through, was to take precautionary measures.

One Friday, in the early afternoon, I decided I should go into the emergency room and see what was going on. I had been feeling weaker and was experiencing dizziness, along with just an overall feeling of not being well. I had lost thirty-five pounds in the last year, going from 155 pounds down to 120 pounds.

Upon my arrival to the hospital, they admitted me in to the ER. As I began to describe the symptoms I was experiencing, they decided to run a few tests, and it was finally determined that I was suffering from malnutrition. After six hours, they admitted me into the hospital and rolled my bed up to a room on the second floor.

By the time I finally got settled into my new hospital room, it was evening, and the halls were quiet. The lights were dimmed, and I was alone as Melody had gone home quite some time ago. I had a roommate, but he was quiet and watching TV.

What happened next was not only alarming but somewhat confusing. A very sharp, good-looking doctor with piercing, beautiful blue eyes came into my room. He was dressed in an expensive black suit with a black shirt and a black tie. This guy was incredibly impressive. He walked up to my bedside, and without introducing himself or making any other comment, he said, "I need to inform you that you only have six months to live," and then he left. As quickly as he entered the room, he left.

I was shocked as one might imagine. Did I hear him right? How could I only have six months to live? Had the cancer come back? My mind was racing, trying to figure out who this doctor was and why he had relayed such a devastating message in such an abrupt manner.

Still reeling from the news, I immediately texted my family and told them what the doctor had said. Although at that time, I didn't reveal anything else about him. Everyone was as shocked as I was to hear the news. It seemed to come so suddenly. But with everything I had been through, nobody really questioned it, they just started praying for God to heal me.

It had only been a few days when I was informed that they needed to transfer me to another room. They had been performing tests to see what was going on with my kidneys since I'd been having trouble urinating during my stay at the hospital. As they probed further, they learned that I had been taking an excessive amount of a vitamin D supplement.

It had been colder-than-usual weather in Seattle, and one of my coworkers suggested I increase the dosage of vitamin D that I was already taking. It was early spring, and the flu season was in full force, so I had increased the amount of IUs significantly, thinking it would help stave off any sickness. Unfortunately, instead of helping me, the excessive amount of vitamin D was causing calcification in my right kidney. Upon the results of their findings, there was a prognosis of kidney disease that would now require a lengthier stay since it was necessary that I undergo treatment.

I called Jill, my younger sister, to tell her about the new findings and to ask her to start praying. I'm not sure how the subject even came about, but while we were talking, I casually mentioned the incident with the doctor in black. As I explained to her in detail what happened, she immediately said, "That was of Satan! No doctor would approach their patient in such a direct and abrupt manner and then leave!"

With what I saw and heard, I completely agreed with her. I had never heard of a doctor's visit where the doctor was dressed in black apparel. And not only that, but the fact that he came into the room and gave me a report of death was also suspicious. I was beginning to wonder what was really going on. This wasn't a vision I'd had; he looked like a real person. We ended our phone conversation, agreeing to pray against the report of death that had been spoken to me.

The next two weeks were spent in the hospital with treatments to deal with the issue in my kidneys. I was also put on a meal plan so I could get the nutrition my body needed to help it heal. Within a couple of weeks, I was at the place where they could release me to go back home. And home never felt so good!

Now, the VA benefits would kick in. I had no idea when three years earlier, through the loss of my job and having to apply for employment benefits, I would be provided with a financial miracle.

Melody and I were not in the position where we could have paid for my two-week hospital stay. With me not working, Melody had taken a job, but her income was barely enough to pay the bills. Not to mention having medical expenses on top of it. Plus, we had no insurance.

My medical expenses for the two-week stay in the hospital, with tests and medications, were astronomical! The average cost for one night's stay in a hospital in Washington in 2013 was $3,361.00. Times that by fourteen, add the emergency room, the tests, and medications. It would have bankrupted us for sure.

But here we were in the place God had already provided for "such a time as this." Three years earlier, the VA had committed to paying one hundred percent of my hospitalization. It was such an amazing realization to think that God had actually planned in advance for this financial need right now. One that we would have never anticipated. One of my favorite promises in the Bible states, "And my God will meet all your needs according to the riches of his glory in Christ Jesus" Philippians 4:19. God's provision along with the timing of it was perfect.

CHAPTER 6

When Plans Change

I think it's accurate to say that many of us have had a plan, or a goal for our lives, that didn't take the path we expected. Personally, I believe it's good to have plans and set goals. It offers purpose and the feeling of accomplishment in our lives. But at the same time, I've learned that it's important to be flexible in the carrying out of my plans and goals. Sometimes, God may have a different plan in mind than the one we had. Proverbs 16:9 says, "In their hearts humans plan their course, but the Lord establishes their steps."

Then there is the timing involved in the plan. Sometimes, it can be very easy to question God's timing. Generally speaking, we're a people who want what we want and would prefer it right now. There are times when it seems as if we're not even on God's clock. Yet, there is never a time in which He is not aware of the desires of our hearts. He does, however, know better than we do, whether what we want to happen is necessary or good for us. His timing and His plans are always perfect.

So many times, we wish things would move along a little more quickly. Impatience seems to be a common attribute of all human beings. Perhaps, we are in a difficult season, just wanting it to be over as soon as possible. It could be a physical malady, a financial upheaval, a relational disruption, or a myriad of other issues in our lives. Though it is natural to want to look ahead, we run the risk of missing the things God needs us to see at this time. Time is never meaningless for Him, and if we try to jump ahead, we may not learn the very lessons that will so benefit us in the season to come. He is not ignoring us when time seems to stand still but rather keeping us in the present so we may prepare for the upcoming season.

God has given so many examples in the Bible of how He changed the plans of man. One such example was of the Apostle Paul when he was on his second missionary journey. He and those that were with him traveled through Phrygia and Galatia, which were north of the Mediterranean Sea, headed for Bithynia. But when they got to Mysia, just a little southwest of their destination, the Holy Spirit stopped them. They weren't allowed to continue with their plan to go to Bithynia. God had another plan for them.

That night, Paul had a vision. In the vision, a man from Macedonia came to him and begged, "Come across to Macedonia and help us." After Paul had seen the vision, they immediately prepared to leave for Macedonia.

Paul said, "We understood that God had called us to tell the Good News to those people." Paul's plan and intentions were good when he desired to go to Bithynia, but that was not the plan God had in mind. So as they were moving toward their goal, God redirected them.

We like to be able to understand the how and why of things that happen in our lives. We want to know what time, where to go, how to get there, and what will happen when we do. It helps us to create a sense of security around our plan. It's a way for us to have some control over the situation. But God's ways and His timing are so far from our own concept that it can be difficult for us not to panic at the thought of trusting Him. When we do, however, we can regain our sense of security by drawing it from its rightful place in Him. When we remain hopeful despite our waiting, God rewards us with renewed strength.

Oh! How we would rather stomp our feet and shout when God doesn't follow our plan. Though we may put our trust in Him, it can be difficult to wait patiently. Waiting *quietly* seems even more difficult. It's not that God cannot handle our outbursts or doesn't want us to be honest with Him, but more that we can learn so much in the quiet. When we seek him with a quieted soul, we can hear the whispers of his goodness all around us. He is speaking, assuring us of His goodness, but we will miss it if we are too loud in the waiting.

I love how God hasn't left us to learn this on our own. He's reminded us over and over, with stories in the Bible, so we can glean from the experiences of others. We can read story after story of people who encountered changes in their plans.

After the glorious exodus from Egypt, the Israelites were "supposed" to walk into the Promise Land—the home long-hoped for. It was only an eleven-mile journey from where they were. However, after thirty-nine years of wandering in the wilderness, it was clear things were not going as they had planned. Their plan was also a good one as they just wanted to be free from slavery to the Egyptians. God had never intended for their journey to take this long. His plan was to do them good. But as time went on, their hearts were tested to see if He could trust them with what He wanted to give them. So we learn from this that the motives of our hearts can be tested while we're waiting.

Mary and Joseph were "supposed" to get married and start a family and lead normal lives—but after an angel showed up with a mission from above, plans changed. Mary, still a virgin, became pregnant with the Son of God. That had certainly never happened before, and one can only imagine what Joseph must have thought. Their plans were now being redirected by God's plan, and it was about to impact them in ways they never imagined! These change in plans required the releasing of their desires to submitting to God's desires.

Lazarus was "supposed" to be healed, after all, he was a close, personal friend with Jesus Himself. But after his sickness took a turn for the worse, suddenly, his family realized plans had changed. Jesus knew that time was of the essence in this situation, yet He waited two more days before even starting the journey to where Lazarus was. And in the meantime, Lazarus died! What kind of friend would do that? God's plan was different than what His friends expected. These change in plans required trusting Him, even though they couldn't see or understand what He was doing.

So many men and women in the Bible didn't understand why God had so drastically changed their plans, and you and I are no different. But God is more concerned with the outcome than the scenario. After all, the scenario is only temporary; outcomes are eternal. He sees beyond what we see and knows what's best for us. Isaiah 55:9 tells us, "As the heavens are higher than the earth, so are My ways higher than your ways and My thoughts than your thoughts." How could we ever think that we know better than God? We read in Romans 11:33, "Oh, the depth of the riches of the wisdom and knowledge of God! How unsearchable His judgments and His paths beyond tracing out!"

It is not our place to tell God what to do. At least, not if we really want what's best for us. His desires for us are good. He is a Father who loves His children and will go to any lengths to prove His love to us. Many of us have had to deal with impossible, difficult situations that were never a part of our plan. Though some of us have never faced changes that required such drastic decisions, still we all have things that didn't work out the way they were "supposed" to. I can most assuredly tell you that getting cancer was never anything I had planned for my life. But life happens, plans change, yet God is still there.

Plans can be good, but when our focus is so intent on making them happen, it can be crushing when things just don't work out like we wanted them to. When our whole life is shaped around our plans, suddenly, we can become so concentrated on accomplishing them that we lose sight of God. Too often, our lives are dedicated to serving our own plans.

But as Christians, we are called to serve only "One." Our plans can become idols. When we live our lives trying to achieve expectations that we have determined the outcome ahead of time, we tend to put our plans above God's. And the thing about our plans is, they can always change. But God never does.

Many times, our plans turn out to be like the house built on sand that Jesus described in Matthew 7:24. When the winds and waves of change come, the house, because it was built on an unstable foundation, crumbles into the sea. But faith in God's eternal purpose is the house built on the rock: "The rain came down, the streams rose, and the winds blew and beat against that house; yet it did not fall, because it had its foundation on the rock."

Tragedies may happen. Winds and waves may roar all around us. We are all human and make mistakes, doing things we regret and then, faced with consequences. But when we rely on God—not on our own ability, to make our plans become realities—things that weren't supposed to happen actually turn out all right. Most plans don't allow for second chances. But God is a God of second chances. And we have His promise that what was meant for evil to bring us harm, God will turn to our good. That very circumstance will turn to become a benefit to us.

Once again, I was about to learn, yet, another lesson as I chose to follow a plan. Mind you, at the time, I thought my choice was lining up with God's plan. Maybe, I didn't inquire of the Lord as to what He wanted. Perhaps, I assumed I was in agreement with His plan. At any rate, I made a decision, and to this day, I'm still not sure if that decision affected the outcome.

My oncology doctor I had been seeing since the beginning of my diagnosis with cancer decided to resign her position at the hospital in order to pursue another opportunity elsewhere. It was in the summer of 2014, and I had been assigned a new oncologist. I was due for a routine check-up to make sure everything was still on course, and I was still in remission. I was a bit surprised when this new doctor recommended I should probably start thinking about having another round of chemotherapy.

At that time, I was taking four or five supplements that claimed cancer cells could not survive in the kind of environment these products would produce. So, I refused my new doctor's suggestion. I figured if the PH balance was in proper order, it was impossible for me to get cancer, so why go through chemotherapy again?

I returned to visit her three months later for again another routine check-up. I had no physical signs in my body that anything had changed concerning the cancer. So I was a bit taken aback when the oncologist suggested for the second time that it might be a good idea to have the chemotherapy treatments. With believing that my body was creating an environment where cancer cells could not grow, I refused the recommendation for a second time.

As time progressed, I would only have to wonder if I had made the right choice. They say hindsight is twenty-twenty, and looking back now, I'm not sure if my decision took me down a path that could have been different. I really don't know. However, what I do know is that God was still in control of my situation, and He promised to work all things for my good. I stood on His promise then, and I still stand on His promise today. "And we know that in all things God works for the good of those who love Him, who have been called according to His purpose" Romans 8:28.

CHAPTER 7

A New Place of Trust

It had been well over a year since my ordeal with kidney damage that had placed me in the hospital and seven years since that first diagnosis of cancer. I had retired, and life had become quite comfortable.

Nearly every morning started with a walk at the marina close by our house. I would go by myself as this was the time I spent talking with the Lord. I never knew what to expect as each day was different. Some days I had questions in which, many times, He gave me answers through things I witnessed while walking along the beach by the water. Other times, I would just spend the morning thanking and praising Him for His goodness. I had been through so much in the past seven years, and many times, I was overwhelmed by all the miracles He had performed in my life.

One morning in December of that same year, as I was walking along the marina, I felt a tug at my heart to begin praying for someone that was going to receive a miracle in 2015. I immediately began talking to the Lord about it. It felt as though He was preparing *me* for something, but I just wasn't sure what. I contacted my sister a few days later since I couldn't shake this thought. It seemed to be getting stronger. When I told her what I had been feeling and praying about, she said that she had been feeling and hearing the same thing from the Lord. We agreed to just keep praying about it and ask the Lord to reveal what it all meant.

When I was talking to my wife about it, she shared that she too had the same impression to pray the same thing. A few days later, speaking with my son, he stated that he was experiencing the same thought and had been praying about it. Four people were praying for someone that was going to receive a miracle in their life that next year. At that point in time, not a single one of us had any idea what that miracle might be, or who would be the recipient.

It was a week or so, after having the initial impression of the miracle, that I was beginning to wonder if God was preparing *me* for something. The more I prayed, the stronger it got. One day, again, while walking on the beach at the marina, the Lord and I were conversing. I must have been asking about the impression I had of a miracle. I don't recall the exact conversation. But what I do remember is He spoke, and with much clarity. It wasn't audible, but it might as well have been. He said, "I love you, Bud, and I will not harm you."

When I talked to my wife, Melody, about what I heard, she expressed that God had been impressing on her heart that I was about to experience something really big. When I was talking with my sister, Jill, just a few days later, she felt that God had been speaking to her the same thing.

Now, while it was a bit exciting to think that God may be getting ready to perform a miracle in my life, there was also some curiosity, especially not knowing what the miracle had to do with. The times spent with the Lord, walking on the beach for the past year, had brought me to a new place in my relationship with Him. It was a new place of total surrender to whatever He desired for my life. I truly trusted Him without reservation. As the days passed, I couldn't help but ponder the thought more and more. It really did feel like God was preparing me for something new . . . different . . . big!

It wasn't but two or three weeks later, on New Year's Day 2015, I was having a strange feeling in my chest. Something just wasn't right. I went to bed that night, thinking that by morning it would be fine. In the middle of the night when I woke up, I was having a difficult time breathing. My chest felt heavy. I would take a breath, but I had to labor to receive the amount of oxygen that I needed. I remained in bed, waiting it out, thinking it was probably just some sort of an abnormality and tried to ignore the symptoms.

I finally realized that it was not going away, and so did my wife. She insisted that I let her take me to the emergency room immediately. I was still breathing heavily when I arrived at the ER. After the preliminary check in, I was taken to a room where they began checking my vitals, drew some blood, and performed some initial tests.

As my breathing continued to be laborious, they discovered that there was fluid in my lungs. So the nurse was instructed to perform a lung draw, where they drained liquid out of my lungs. Once that procedure was over, I felt a little relief, but I was still in quite a bit of pain.

Both Melody and I were quite surprised when they came in and said I could go home. In fact, I was a little irritated with their decision because I felt like they hadn't really dug deep enough yet to find out what was really going on. It took me back to when the Swedish hospital lost all my biopsy information. It was as if it was no big deal, just go home and everything will be okay. When I tried to express my concern, the nurse just had a flippant attitude and insisted I could be released to go home.

The next day, I resumed my normal activities at home. I still hurt, but figured since the medical staff wasn't concerned, I shouldn't be either. After about a week, I knew something was not right, especially since in the last few days, my breathing had gotten worse and worse.

Late Saturday afternoon, on January 10, I was having a difficult time inhaling, and it had become very painful just to breathe. My mother-in-law lived in the basement apartment of our home as she had severe dementia, and my wife was her caregiver. Many times, I would go downstairs to help attend to her needs. But with each time, walking back upstairs to where my wife and I lived, I felt more winded. I could tell that I was having an unusually difficult time breathing. I am the type of person that is so optimistic, that I think everything will eventually work itself out. But this time, my breathing had become so laborious, I could hardly catch my breath. That's when I knew my wife needed to get me to the hospital.

As we began walking to the car, I felt like I wasn't going to make it. My mother-in-law was on oxygen twenty-four hours a day and had a supply of oxygen bottles. So, I asked my wife to go downstairs and see if I could use one of her bottles, at least until I got to the hospital. She left to go find out from her mom if that would be okay and quickly returned with a bottle and a set of oxygen tubes. Immediately, I got everything hooked up and began using the oxygen so I could make it to the car.

Upon arriving at the emergency room, they admitted me promptly and gave me a room. A routine exam was performed, and it was soon determined that I needed a thoracentesis, which is also known as a pleural tap or a lung draw. It's a procedure done when there's too much fluid in the pleural space, a small space between the lungs and the chest wall. The fluid is then analyzed to figure out the cause of the fluid accumulation around the lungs. It was at this same time that they ended up draining one-and-a-half liters of fluid from my lungs and decided to admit me into the hospital. They also informed me that if I had waited another twenty-four hours to come in to the hospital, I would have drowned from the liquid in my lungs!

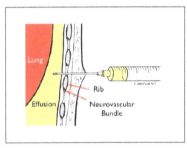 

I was transferred from the ER to a room in the hospital, and just as usual, it took some time for them to get me settled in. I was feeling relief from the draining of fluid from my lungs, but I was still far from comfortable. Later that night, they began checking my lungs for blood clots.

The next few days were very uncertain as they continued to drain the fluid that continually kept filling my lungs. They also found during this time that my lymph nodes were growing. The doctors were blaming everything that was happening on the lymph nodes! It was scary since I'd already had cancer once, and the lymph nodes were all a part of that. I wasn't sure what to think or do, so Melody and I prayed and asked the Lord for wisdom. We also started texting family members of what had transpired so they could begin praying with us.

I had been keeping in touch with my son, Gabe, and my daughter, Shawna. By now, they were extremely concerned because it didn't seem like the doctors had any affirmative answers. On Tuesday, January 13, the kids decided to make a trip up to hospital from their homes in the Portland, Oregon area. My whole family was beginning to get concerned as well and, one by one, began calling to find out how I was doing.

That morning, Jill called to check in with me. All I could tell her was that we were just waiting for answers. I think she was somewhat relieved when she was able to hear my voice; I was tired, but under the circumstances, I was doing pretty good. In fact, I had enough energy that I was going to get up and take a shower.

They drained another liter of fluid from my lungs as this had been a common procedure most every day since the day I had arrived at the ER. I was scheduled for a biopsy on my lymph nodes. But the doctors were still a little baffled at this point because they couldn't find anything else wrong, just that the lymph nodes were growing.

An oncologist was scheduled to come in and see me later that afternoon, so I was at least hoping that he may be able to give me some answers. I wasn't discouraged by any means. I just wanted some answers. And as I had thought back to what the Lord had told me and the other three family members just a month earlier, *I knew there was going to be a miracle in this in the end.*

Shawna and Gabe arrived at the hospital about two-forty-five that afternoon. It turned out, God's timing for them was perfect, because about three-thirty, the doctor everyone had been waiting to hear from came into my room and gave us all a complete rundown of what was going on with my body.

The diagnosis was in. It was an *aggressive* type of cancer . . .

Once the doctor left, I knew the kids were concerned, especially Shawna. She had just gone through this with her son, who had Leukemia, and now it was her dad with aggressive lymphoma. I wanted to reach out and comfort her and tell her it was going to be okay. But her emotions were still raw as I knew she was trying to figure out how she was going to get through this.

I asked Gabe to please let the rest of the family know. He put together an email and sent it out to each family member:

"As you might imagine, Dad was upbeat when the doctor shared the news about the cancer. We prayed together and talked about God plans in all of this. Dad talked about how amazing it was,] that we were all there when the doctors came in to share the news. He is ready to tackle this challenge, and he's relying on God's power and all our prayers and support to get him through."

"The Dr.'s diagnosis: Follicular lymphoma. This is the type of lymphoma that Dad has had from 2008. The doctors say this lymphoma is likely to stay with him although it is a slow, growing cancer.

"Diffuse large B-Cell lymphoma (DLBCL), this is the new type of lymphoma Dad has. It is much more aggressive. The fluid around his lungs was discovered to be basically the cells of this cancer. That is why the chemo will be more intense this time.

"So, what's next? First, Dad will have a heart scan to be sure that his heart is ready for the treatment. Then he will have a pick line installed to make the treatments easier for him to receive. Next, he will start the first of six cycles of chemo this Friday. These are three-week cycles. They will stop to evaluate after the first three cycles to make sure everything, is going well."

The doctor's report had not been what we desired to hear. And it certainly wasn't our plan for me to have a cancer a second time. But I wasn't panicked this time. It felt as though I had somehow been prepared for this moment in time. I had a peace, knowing that God had a specific plan in this, and I expressed it to the rest of my family.

Once again, I went back to what God had spoken just a few weeks earlier, that He was going to perform a miracle for someone in 2015,and that He loved me and wouldn't harm me. This was *His plan*. I didn't try to figure out what He was going to do, or how He was going to do it. I just knew He was leading in this and all I had to do was follow.

I knew that I was going to be healed, even though I didn't know how God was going to choose to do that. After having gone through the bout of cancer, malnutrition, kidney damage, and the effects of chemotherapy, one thing I was sure of was that nothing was impossible with God. He had been teaching me about faith and healing, and here I was again, at that specific moment, where He had the opportunity to prove Himself to be true to His Word.

CHAPTER 8

God's Healing Power

The New Testament is full of stories that give proof of God's healing power. As we read the first four gospels of Matthew, Mark, Luke, and John, it's interesting to find that everywhere Jesus went, He healed and cast out demons. He saw their needs and had compassion on them. Shouldn't it be the same for us today?

Why do we question whether or not it is God's will to heal? I'm reminded of the story in Matthew 8:1–3, "When Jesus came down from the mountainside and large crowds followed Him. A man with leprosy came and knelt before Him and asked, 'Lord, if You are *willing*, You, can make me clean.' Jesus reached out His hand and touched the man, '*I am willing,*' He said. 'Be clean!' *Immediately, he was cleansed of his leprosy.*" (Italics are my own emphasis).

In Mark 5:25–34, we read of another instance where Jesus healed, however, the circumstances were entirely different this time. A woman was in His presence, who had been subject to bleeding for twelve years. She had suffered a great deal under the care of many doctors and had spent all she had, *yet instead of getting better, she grew worse*.

When she heard about Jesus, she came up behind him in the crowd and touched his cloak *because she thought*, "If I just touch his clothes, I will be healed." Immediately, her bleeding stopped, and she felt in her body that she was freed from her suffering. *At once, Jesus realized that power had gone out from him*. He turned around in the crowd and asked, "Who touched my clothes?" "You see the people crowding against you," his disciples answered, "and yet you can ask,

'Who touched me?' But Jesus kept looking around to see who had done it.

Then the woman, knowing what had happened to her, came and fell at his feet and, trembling with fear, told him the whole truth. He said to her, "Daughter, *your faith has healed you*. Go in peace and be freed from your suffering."

Why do we try and put God in a box, as if to figure out that there is a certain way He wants to do a thing in us? What if He just desires to heal us? That's it! In the first story, the man asked Jesus if He was *willing* to heal him. Jesus *was willing,* and the man was healed.

In the second story, Jesus was actually tending to another request from a man named Jairus to come and heal his sick daughter. It was while He was on His way to fulfill another man's desire that He was interrupted by this woman who needed Jesus's help. Her thought was that if she could just touch the hem of His garment, she would be healed. She *knew* Jesus didn't even have to be aware of her need; all she had to do was believe and draw His healing power from Him. What happened that caused the healing power of Jesus to be released from Him, without Him saying He was willing, like in the first story?

Jesus, when He felt the healing virtue being released from Him, knew that someone's faith had just pulled it from Him. He said, "Daughter, *your faith* has healed you." Notice, He didn't say, "Because I am willing," nor did He say, "Because of your faith, *'I'* have healed you." He told her, "*Your* faith has healed you. Go in peace and be freed from your suffering."

"Coming to his hometown, Jesus began teaching the people in their synagogue, and they were amazed. 'Where did this man get this wisdom and these miraculous powers?' they asked. 'Isn't this the carpenter's son? Isn't his mother's name, Mary, and aren't his brothers James, Joseph, Simon, and Judas? Aren't all his sisters with us? Where then did this man get all these things?' And they took offense at him. But Jesus said to them, 'A prophet is not without honor except in his own town and in his own home.' And he did not do many miracles there *because of their lack of faith*." (Italics are my emphasis).

So, how does this whole healing idea work? According to what I've read in His Word and experienced in my own life, it's all about faith. But one says, "I've been sick for many years, and God hasn't healed me. I *do have faith and believe, and yet, God has not desired to heal me.*" I honestly do not have the answer for that. I have my own opinions and beliefs, but God has not asked me to give my opinions but only to share His Word.

I do encourage each reader at this place to inquire of the Lord for yourself to find out what His intentions are toward you in your present circumstance. I also want to encourage you, that while you may be sick and in need of healing, to embrace Jesus and His desire for you rather than embracing the illness.

I agree that we all have a "place of suffering" as we walk this journey with Jesus. Yes, Paul was given a "thorn in his flesh," although we don't have proof of what exactly that might have been. Job was tested with physical ailments, as Satan was given permission by the Lord to test him. We are also told that Jesus learned obedience through the things which He suffered. However, there is not one incident mentioned as to Him ever being sick.

So please, lay aside the mindsets you may have at this present time and take your questions to the Lord. Don't walk away until He answers. In humility, submitting yourself to Him, ask Him, "What are your intentions toward me in this circumstance I'm facing?" If you truly put your faith in Him, trusting that He will give you understanding according to His will, His wishes and desires for you, He will answer.

Our Heavenly Father loves us more than we can even comprehend. He desires that we know Him and follow Him. He desires more than we can imagine that we come to know Him and His ways, not just what He can do for us. What father gives his child a stone when he asks for bread?

So once again, with an earnest and sincere plea to each and every reader who questions what their Heavenly Father has in store for them personally, seek Him and you will find Him as you seek Him with your whole heart. Lay aside your "what ifs," your "but I always thought," your "but I already have," your "but what if it doesn't work," your fears, your ideas, and your thoughts. Allow your Heavenly Father the opportunity to speak into your situation and over your life. Have faith and trust in Him that He will work all things to your good according to His purpose. He has a plan for you, and He is working that plan in and through you, whether you see it or not.

I was totally convinced that the Lord had something mighty planned in everything that was happening to me. I had begun sharing my faith and what I believed God was about to do in healing my body with every medical staff member that came into my room.

As nightfall approached, I had been lying in bed for quite a while, listening to my roommate sing out loud. I was sure he must have been a Christian because He was singing Christian songs. I couldn't get to sleep, and at some time during the middle of the night, I got up to go to the bathroom. On my way back to my bed, the gentleman in the bed next to mine asked me if he could pray for me. I was more than willing to have a prayer said in my behalf. I stood there as he prayed, and when he was finished, I got back into bed and was soon asleep.

The next morning on Thursday, January 15, the nurses assigned to my room were in and out, checking on me. I really hadn't been feeling well all morning. They had commented that it looked like they were going to have to start an intensive chemotherapy treatment for me. But before that could happen, they would have to move me from the sixth floor down to the second floor, which is where I would be receiving the treatment. They were just waiting for a bed to come available. In the meantime, they did another drain from my lungs and started preparing me for the move.

Before long, I was making the trip down to my "new home" on the second floor. My new room was beautiful. The view was amazing as it encompassed the entire city of Seattle. I was thoroughly enjoying my new room with the view when the nurse came in and informed me I was scheduled for my first round of chemotherapy, beginning the next evening at seven. It sounded like everything was moving along smoothly.

The love and support from my family was overwhelmingly abundant! I was settling in when Gabe, his wife, Melissa, and their oldest son, Dawson, came to visit me. We enjoyed talking together about God's goodness through this entire ordeal. Our hearts were filled with gratitude for what He had done in spite of what we knew might be ahead. They didn't stay long, but it had been so enjoyable having them there with me.

A little later, my sister-in-law, Linda, called to see how I was doing. I was able to give her a report of feeling somewhat tired, but overall, I was doing good. Even though I had been in quite a bit of pain over the previous night, I was doing better as the day went on. I expressed how much peace I was feeling and that I knew God had this. As we ended the call, I thanked her for everyone's concern and prayers for me and added, "I'm hoping to be able to watch the Seahawk game on Sunday!"

My brother, Bruce, called later that evening, and as we talked about the chemo treatments, I explained to him that they were going to be "*turbo*" chemotherapy treatments. He told me I needed to read "today's" devotional in the Jesus Calling book. He said that it was written just for me, for "today," and it would put a smile on my face. At that, we ended the call, and he assured me that everyone was praying.

I really had no idea what to expect next. I thought it would be like the chemo treatments I'd received in 2008. So I had envisioned that I would have the first round of chemo on Friday, then end with the second treatment on Saturday, and be released to go home. I was aware that if it was anything like the chemotherapy treatments I'd had in 2008, it would take two days before I got really sick and then I would be fine. Following that, I would go back in a month later and do it again. Just a week earlier, Bruce and I had made plans to go to a King's Garden High School basketball game in February, and we were still planning on doing that!

Jill also called me, and as usual, our conversation was extremely uplifting. I don't know what it is about our relationship, but it's more than just brother and sister; we have that brother-and-sister-in-Christ relationship. We are always on the same page spiritually.

The next morning, she had relayed to the family, "I got to talk to Bud last night. He sounded weak but good. I was so encouraged after our conversation. It's amazing how he's the one suffering and he encouraged me! God has a miraculous plan in all of this. We just don't know how many lives are going to be touched and changed through this. Bud's willingness to endure this is an absolute testimony to the grace God gives us."

And the next morning, I awoke feeling pretty good. I was looking forward to getting the first chemotherapy treatment behind me and felt encouraged in my spirit. But as the day progressed, my lungs were filling with fluid. It was getting more and more uncomfortable as I was having difficulty breathing again.

My younger sister, Jill, had called a few hours before I was due to begin my treatment, but I had to cut the call extremely short as I was so out of breath and could hardly talk. I knew my older sister, Jackie, would be calling soon as well, so to avoid speaking, I just informed her I was okay, and then I texted her, "Another amazing journey. Pretty uncomfortable but so was the cross. I can't talk on the phone because I lose breath too easily."

As late afternoon was approaching, they performed another lung drain. That procedure always helped my lungs feel better and my breathing to become less laborious. By that time, I was pretty worn out, so I rested until my chemo treatment at 7:00 p.m. It had been brutal, but God was still good!

It had seemed like a very long day. Maybe because I was anticipating the treatment and looking forward to it being over. But before long, the chemotherapy treatment had been completed, and having been in and out of consciousness somewhere during this time frame, I had entered in to a spiritual vision. It was at this time I began seeing the following scenario take place. Immediately, I thought these things were happening in real time.

In this vision, Melody had taken me to the hospital, and I was being admitted into the hospital. For some reason, it was taking longer than usual to get the paperwork done for my admission. Normally, I was questioned on a few items, then I would get some blood work done as well as my vital signs. It rarely took more than a few minutes, so I couldn't understand "why the waiting game."

I was getting tired and a little impatient when I noticed a wooden bench with wooden slats. It looked like it might be a good place to lie down even though it looked very uncomfortable. Melody and I had only been there a short time when I gave in to fatigue and found my way over to the bench. Within minutes, a nurse came over and said that my attitude was unacceptable, and I needed to follow her to another room.

I didn't understand as I hadn't even talked to anyone. I tried to convince her I was just resting for a few minutes until my wife could help me to wherever I was to go next. That made things even worse. She escorted me forcibly to another floor and into a room by myself. I kept wondering where Melody was and how I was going to let her know where they had moved me, or was the nurse going to do that for me?

I wasn't in that room, but about thirty minutes when they shuffled me off to another room with other patients. Instead of beds, there were cots on the floor resembling army cots. The room reminded me of an open barracks, a FEMA camp or a triage. I was very uncomfortable with where I was and why I had been taken there.

They got me situated and gave me a warm blanket as I had requested. The room was extremely cold. After lying down for about ten minutes, another nurse came in to the room and placed an IV in my right arm. I started looking around because the environment was not like any hospital I had ever seen. Now I wasn't seeing any other cots, so it didn't make sense to me.

I began to jostle around because I was uncomfortable, both physically and emotionally, and it aroused the attention of the nurse. She was not very attentive or accommodating to my needs and expected me to deal with my discomfort. I was getting a little irritated. As I was trying to reach for some water, I turned to the nurse that put the IV into my arm and asked if I could have something to drink. She brought me a liter of cold water in a yellow pitcher, and from what I was observing, she was not happy. As a matter of fact, I'd never been treated like this in any hospital that I had ever been in.

When she came over to me in her anger, she pulled the IV out of my arm and blamed me for pulling it out, making a scene, so the other nurses on the floor could hear our argument. They all began blaming me and yelling at me.

That got the attention of the lead nurse, who came over to see what the ruckus was all about. The nurse that tore the IV out of my arm told her everything was fine, so the lead nurse left and went to another room. When she left, I struck up a conversation with a different nurse that had entered the area where I was lying. She was a friendly nurse, and I told her that one of the nurses ripped the IV out of my arm. I even showed her the bloody wound where the IV had been placed.

The first nurse that had taken me from the admission area and lead me to the barracks style room where I was now had returned. She had a pair of thick gloves which were placed on my hands so that I couldn't grab anything. This was very scary because I felt like I was being imprisoned and had no freedom to move around.

My mind began racing. Not only was I stuck here, but again, Melody was not near me, and I had no way of contacting her. I was frightened by all of this, and my heart began to pound.

All of a sudden, I heard a loud explosion. I tried to sit up but couldn't. The only thing I could manage to do was raise up far enough to look around and see if anyone else heard it. No one seemed to be astonished by it, so I just lay back down and stayed still. A little later, I heard another loud "boom." It began to concern me that I was hearing noises, and yet, no one else seemed to be hearing them. Another one went off, and again, no one seemed to hear it. By the third one, I had assumed they must be bombs that were going off.

I had heard bombs go off at a distance when I was in the Navy, and they would do drills that would simulate a wartime scenario. The advantage at that time was I knew it was not real. This time, I didn't know if it was real, a drill, or my imagination. In my mind, someone was bombing the hospital. At least, that's what I had surmised.

I called the nurse over to my cot and asked her if she had heard the noises. Her unconcerned response was, "Don't worry, everything is okay."

But by this time, I had somehow envisioned that the VA Hospital was on the top of a hill and that planes were flying overhead. I could hear them and envisioned that planes were coming from down below the hill, flying overhead, and bombs were being launched toward us. I was convinced because that was what I was hearing. Another one went off, and I was ready to get out of there.

The nurse came over and asked me if I was scared. I said, "No, I am a Christian, and God has everything under control," at which she nodded in agreement. That gave me the idea that maybe she, too, was a Christian, so I asked her, "Are you a Christian?" She again gave a half-hearted nod and left.

I began praying, "God, keep us all safe." Although it helped settle my emotions, the sounds of bombing continued. Again, I looked around. At the end of the long room were other male nurses going about their regular routine, as if nothing was out of the ordinary. Even though I had settled down a little, I was still very concerned.

My attention turned to the area I was in, and I could hear the nurse that didn't seem to like me talking to other nurses. When they came over to my cot, I was told to get up because they were going to move me to yet, another room.

I was extremely confused at everything that was transpiring. I still hadn't been able to talk to Melody, and they hadn't given me any information as to when I would be able to see her. I asked them if I could see my wife, and they said she was still filling out paperwork. That was very confusing to me as I had been there for quite a while, and I couldn't understand why it would take her that long to fill out paperwork. My suspicious mind began going crazy.

The nurses hurriedly helped me out of bed, and we walked into another room. This one was much better because there was a real bed, and it was a private room.

One of the male nurses that had been talking with the female nurse that didn't seem to like me was now my new nurse. Before he came into my new room, I had heard the two of them talking outside the door of my room. The *mean* nurse said to him in a mocking tone of voice, "Oh, he says he's had a religious experience." And they both laughed.

During the entire shift that he was my nurse, he seemed very gruff, only doing the very minimum, such as taking my vitals, checking my saline fluids, and looking in on me once in a while. I had asked him for a warm blanket, and it took a long time before I was attended to. That was just another indication of his attitude.

It seemed strange, but they were in the planning stages of giving me another private room in the intensive care unit. I couldn't understand why I was being moved from room to room. When a male nurse came to transport me, I heard a conversation stating that I claimed to be a Christian and didn't deserve to be in the same area as other patients. Was I undergoing some kind of persecution for my faith?

I could turn my head and see the nurses station where they were training new nurses, and it was also within hearing distance. Between the way they were treating these new nurses and the way they were talking to them, it upset me. I had been a district sales manager for a sales company, and I had trained many people. I knew that a trainee learns best with some understanding.

Without any restraint, I blurted out to the nurse how I thought their training program was not the best way to train. *That* didn't go over too well. If I thought they were not paying attention to me before, now they totally shunned me.

As quickly as the vision had begun, it stopped. All throughout that night and into Saturday, I was feeling panicked and confused. I knew I was in pain and feeling extremely uncomfortable. However, it was almost as though I was in a different world. It was like going in and out of reality; I'm not even sure how to explain it. I just knew that things weren't right, but I couldn't figure out what was happening.

While I was in the vision, I was actually still on the second floor at the Chemotherapy Unit. It was six-forty-five in the evening of

January 17, and I was still in pain and couldn't breathe. I'm pretty sure, by then, I'd already had my second chemotherapy treatment, and my pulse had gradually increased, and I had become more restless. I'd had a difficult time remaining still in bed. At 9:43 p.m., due to the pain, they gave me morphine. At that time, my pulse had increased to one hundred and forty beats per minute. The doctor that was in the room to re-evaluate me said that my condition had changed and now required closer monitoring. Apparently, my condition had shown no improvement throughout the night.

According to the medical records, the medical staff was very concerned that I might have Sepsis, an illness in which the body has a severe inflammatory reaction to bacteria or other germs. It carries the potential of being life-threatening.

The next morning, which was Sunday, January 18 at 7:30 a.m., a code blue (cardiac arrest) was called. According to the medical records, I was intubated (had a breathing tube inserted), and there was no pulse. I had flat-lined at that point. After five minutes of trying to revive me, they regained a pulse, and I was immediately transferred to the ICU floor. My heart had stopped, my kidneys had failed, and I had stopped breathing on my own. I was now hooked up to life-supporting machines.

As soon as I reached the intensive care unit, a doctor contacted Melody and described to her what had just happened, that I had died and they were able to revive me, but I was on life support, and she needed to get to the hospital immediately. She was already in route to visit me when they called.

Melody immediately contacted Gabe to inform him of my condition and asked him to tell Shawna and let her know what had happened. She told Gabe that he and Shawna needed to get to the hospital right away.

Gabe was the pastor of a church in Aloha, Oregon, and was getting ready for his usual Sunday morning message. He immediately made a call and arranged for someone else to lead the service that morning. Shawna, being a mother of four, had to make sure that her husband would be okay with taking care of the children indefinitely. Neither of them knew how long they were going to have to stay in

Seattle. Bruce was also notified, so he and Linda could come to the hospital. Between Shawna and Melody, the rest of the family were notified.

Melody was the first to arrive at the hospital, but not having any idea as to what was going on, she thought I was still in my room on the second floor. Imagine the panic she felt to discover I wasn't in the room. The bed had been made, the room was cleaned and prepared for a new patient. She frantically ran to the nurse's station to find out what had happened to me. By now, she was in tears, thinking the worse. Had I died while she was on her way to the hospital, and they just didn't tell her? As soon as a nurse was located, Melody was finally informed that I had been transferred to the ICU.

Melody was not prepared for what she was about to witness. Her world was about to change, and that change was going to be drastic.

CHAPTER 9

On the Outside Looking In

Bud had entered into a comatose state. It had been just a little over an hour since the doctors, for five long-drawn-out minutes, had been frantically trying to revive him back to life. According to the medical records, he had suffered an acute heart attack and flat-lined. He was now being kept alive through mechanical life support systems. No one was sure at this time if he would live, or if he would die.

As soon as Melody arrived in Bud's room in the ICU, she witnessed her husband in the most distressed manner she had ever seen. To think when she had gotten up that morning, she had planned to visit with him in his hospital room, but here they were now; everything had changed, and all too suddenly.

The first sight she witnessed, as she entered his room, was his mouth opened and tubes stuck down his throat. There were monitors hooked to his body from both sides of the bed. There were the sounds of machines running and beeping, as they were monitoring every breath and heartbeat. He was on *life support. The only thing keeping him alive at this point were the machines all around him.* His body had become swollen, four to five times of what it should have been, and he had no color. Melody was in shock! So many questions racing through her mind. How did this happen? What was the cause? Bud, lying there in bed, limp and totally unaware of anything that was going on.

As Melody watched her husband's lifeless body, lying in that hospital bed, she drew closer to him and began whispering in his ear. But there was no response. She could only hope and pray that everybody would be there soon. It was too quiet. Except for the sounds of the machines, it was just her, Bud, and God. As she sat quietly and watched the breathing machine give her husband a breath, she could see his chest rise, and then it would go down again as the air was released. The reality of his condition was beginning to settle in as she continued observing the rise of his chest, with air going into his lungs and his chest, releasing the air, all because of a machine.

She looked over at the machine that was monitoring his heart and causing it to continue to beat. With each pulse, she realized how dependent his life was on that machine. There was nothing she could do, except wait. And as she waited, she was constantly being reminded by the different rhythmic patterns she was hearing, that each breath and each beat of the heart was being determined and giving life to her husband.

The minutes seemed like hours as she sat by his side, watching and waiting to see if he would wake up. It was during those quiet moments that God began to encourage and strengthen Melody in her spirit. She could literally *feel* God ministering to her. She remembered what God had told them, that Bud was going to experience a miracle, that He loved Bud and would not harm him. Her faith began to increase with each word spoken to God as she pleaded for her husband's life and healing. Somehow, she *knew, He was listening.* What a precious and life-changing moment, just the three of them, sitting in a room, while God in His infinite wisdom planted that seed of faith in the soil of Melody's heart. This was His plan, and one day, they would understand.

So much was going on behind the scenes. It was at the same time as Melody was sitting at Bud's bedside that Jill wrote an email and sent it to each member of the family. God had awakened her at five-thirty that morning; she wasn't sure why she was feeling the draw to Him, but in obedience, she got out of bed and picked up her Bible. She had been reading the Psalms in her daily reading and the next chapters were 118 and 119. So, that's where she turned to read. As soon as she began, she realized that the verses which were standing out to her were verses of life and not death. So, at five-thirty, without having any knowledge that Bud was about to die, she began to pray these prayers as petitions to God on his behalf.

Her e-mail was written as follows:

> These are the verses God had me pray for Bud this morning before I knew what was going on with him. Please agree in prayer for him. I asked Melody to read these Scriptures to Bud so that they will get into His mind and spirit.
>
> "*I shall not die but live and shall declare the works and recount the illustrious acts of the Lord*" (Ps. 118:17).

"This is from the Lord and is His Doings, it is marvelous in our eyes. This is the day which the Lord has brought about; we will rejoice and be glad in it" (Ps. 118:23, 24).

"Turn away my eyes from vanity and restore me to vigorous life and health in your ways. Establish Your Word and confirm your promise to Your servant, which is for those who reverently fear and devotedly worship You" (Ps. 119:37, 38).

"I hate the thoughts of undecided double-minded people, but Your Law I do love. You are my Hiding Place and my Shield; I hope in Your Word" Ps. 119:113, 114).

"Plead my cause and redeem me; revive me and give me life according to Your Word" (Ps. 119:154).

"Great are Your Tender Mercy and Loving-Kindness O Lord, give me life according to Your Ordinance" (Ps. 119:156).

"Consider how I love Your Precepts; revive me and give life to me O Lord, according to Your Loving-Kindness" (Ps. 119:159).

This is all new for me as God is teaching me to *stand on His Word*. In Mark 16:20–24, Jesus clearly states what we are to do when asking something of Him in faith: "In the morning, when they were passing along, they noticed that the fig tree was withered completely away to its roots. And Peter remembered and said to Him, 'Master, look! The fig tree which you cursed has withered away!'

"And Jesus, replying, said to them, 'Have faith in God. Truly, I tell you, whoever says to this mountain, be lifted up, and thrown into the sea! And does not doubt at all in his heart, but believes that what he says will take place, it will be done for him. For this reason, I am telling you, whatever you ask for in prayer, believe that it is granted to you, and you will have it.'"

Well, while I am writing this, I am hearing a voice telling me I will look like a fool if this doesn't come to pass. I have had feelings of fear telling me I am going to look like a fool if God does not heal Bud. This is the voice of the adversary, who wants to kill, steal, and destroy. I will believe the report of the Lord!

Be encouraged, stand steadfast, and pray in faith for Bud's healing. This day, God has called me to fast, pray, and stand. The word that kept coming to me was from the story of Lazarus. 'This sickness is not unto death.

God had already begun making His plan known, but sometimes, faith is a funny thing for us to grasp. We *want* to believe, but when our natural eyes "see" that things are not in agreement with what we're believing for, we start to doubt.

Time had gone extremely slow for Melody as she waited for the others to get to the hospital. She was really feeling the need for some support. Gabe and Shawna finally arrived around five-thirty in the late afternoon and quietly entered the room where their dad was hooked up to life support. How does a child cope with not knowing if their dad is going to live or die? They were witnessing the exact same scene that Melody had witnessed just hours earlier. Someone can tell you about it, but you can't even imagine the horrific sights and sounds and smells of that room, unless you experience it for yourself. And here they were, for the first time, since they had left the hospital with high hopes just a few days earlier.

Bud had been unconscious and unresponsive all day. Melody had been talking to him, but he had not responded. The nurses had been in and out of the room throughout the day. He woke up for a minute while they were doing a procedure and was able to follow commands, which was an encouraging sign because they were worried about his brain function. But once the procedure was over, he had become unresponsive again.

As the three of them began speaking to him, there was still no response. Melody first, Gabe next, and then Shawna. Much to everyone's surprise, as Shawna leaned over and spoke into her dad's ear, he opened his eyes! All three of them witnessed what had just happened, and they began to get excited! So, Melody leaned over and whispered in his ear but no response. They told Gabe to try it, so he did but again, no response. They were all beginning to think that this was just a one-time fluke, kind of like the response the nurse got earlier. That is, until Shawna leaned close and spoke into his ear, and his eyes opened again! It happened over and over! For some unknown reason, he was responding to Shawna's voice.

That was the first time Bud had continued to respond to anyone. It was just a little more evidence that there *was* life in him. They read the Scriptures to him about healing and living, not dying, and had also brought a CD player and worship music. They were all very surprised to see him raise his hands in worship to His Lord as the worship music played. Again, that was even more proof that Bud was alive!

While they were waiting together in his room and the nurses had been in and out, the doctor finally arrived to check on Bud. As they spoke with the doctor, he told them that everything was still up in the air at that time. They didn't really have any answers yet. He reiterated that Bud's kidneys, lungs, and heart had stopped that morning, and they had to perform CPR on him for five minutes to revive him. They weren't sure what damage had been done, or how he was going to recover.

The doctor implied that they still didn't know why any of it happened. They didn't know why his lungs kept filling up, but they would continue draining them as needed. Their plan was to start dialysis soon for his kidneys. He reminded them that those three organs weren't functioning on their own and said, if they unhooked him from all the support, he would die, and they wouldn't be able to bring him back.

It was at that time that the seriousness of what was going on would be revealed. When the doctor was asked what the family could expect in the days to come, his report was beyond disturbing. Bud had been dead for five minutes, allowing the brain to have no oxygen during that time. That had the potential to cause brain damage. The doctor warned that Bud had about a 30 percent chance of living and probably would not make it. And if he did, he would be in a nursing home for the rest of his life. The outlook was bleak, to say the least.

Bruce and Linda had also arrived during this time and were able to hear the reports and see for themselves what was happening with Bud. It was pretty amazing how God continued to speak to the family members. Everyone was still believing for healing. And as Bruce was considering all that had happened and was praying, he was reminded of Hezekiah when he asked the Lord for fifteen more years. God was continually giving His words of life to the family, encouraging each one to not give up on their faith. It had been a while since everyone had arrived, and they were starting to feel a bit hungry. So, they decided to go down to the hospital cafeteria to get a bite to eat. When they were all sitting down to the table and beginning to eat, a man entered the cafeteria. Bruce thought he looked homeless, but Linda thought he looked like a mountain man.

He said he had just been carjacked and asked if anybody had seventy-five cents. Bruce took a dollar out of his wallet and gave it to him. As the man started to walk away, Bruce said, "Jesus loves you!"

He turned around with a *big* smile on his face and asked them, "What is your situation?" Gabe began explaining to him all that had happened to his dad. The man asked if he could pray with them and got down on his knees. They all got in a circle to join him and held hands.

He said to them, "There is going to be a miracle in this." Then he began to tell a story about the Black Plague and how it was incurable. After that, he prayed. He told Gabe to read Ephesians to his dad. Then, the man got up and started to leave, and as he was walking away from them, Bruce called out, "What is your name?"

He turned around and said, "Silence." Then he left.

They were all in amazement, wondering, "Had that been an angel?"

They sat quietly, for a moment, around the table, trying to figure out what had just taken place. As they began talking about what they'd just witnessed, each one of them was convinced that the man named Silence had been sent by God. Whether or not he was angel was still unknown, but they were almost sure he must have been. They recounted the verse in Hebrews that says, "Do not forget to show hospitality to strangers, for by so doing some people have shown hospitality to angels without knowing it" Hebrews 13:2.

It wouldn't be long until Bruce and Linda would have to be returning home, so they all headed for Bud's room. They prayed for him once again, then Bruce and Linda left. Gabe and Shawna had decided to stay at the hospital for another night to wait and see how their dad would do once the dialysis kicked in and his lungs were cleared out again. They didn't feel right about leaving without answers. Melody had to return home to relieve her cousin from caring for Melody's mom but would return first thing in the morning.

Bud was left in his room under the care of the nurses and doctors, but he wasn't alone; God was with him. By now, people from all over the world were praying for his healing. God was listening. God was watching.

CHAPTER 10

Assignment Canceled

It had been within the past thirty-six hours during Bud's comatose state, that he seemed to be in a different realm. While he wasn't aware of the reality of what was happening in the physical world, he was very aware of what was taking place in the spiritual world. While his physical body was reacting negatively, his mind was being invaded with corresponding thoughts of what the enemy's plans were, and that was to take his life. It is here that he begins to convey the strategies and plans as he saw them unfold.

When the nurses began my first chemotherapy treatment, for some reason, it had thrown me into a mental state of confusion and panic. I was wondering, where I was. Why was I lying in a hospital bed? How had I ended up there, and where was Melody? Confusion overwhelmed me, and I began freaking out. I'm not the kind of person that gets scared or worried when an emergency arises; I usually go into a very focused mode. But here I was, starting to feel all those emotions, and I couldn't seem to get them under control. It was cold, and confusion had taken over my mind. Melody, who is normally always by my side, wasn't there.

It wasn't long until I heard a female voice at the end of the intensive care unit. She asked the male nurse if she could see me. This was the same young blonde lady that I had seen at the front desk of the admissions department downstairs when I was admitted in to the hospital. She had been so friendly and had such a bubbly personality. They had allowed her to come in and see me. She was again, very cordial, and in a tone of curiosity yet concern, she asked, "How are you doing?"

I responded, "I'm doing okay, but I feel very tired and confused."

As she questioned me, I began realizing she was more concerned than curious. "I heard that you weren't doing very well, so that's why I came up to check on you. What happened?"

As our conversation continued, I told her I didn't know. I had become very disoriented, so I asked her where I was, and she said I had been transferred to the ICU and that's why she was there. We chatted for a few more minutes and then she left.

It was at that time I heard a male nurse talking in a gruff-sounding voice. "Now, we'll have to get rid of her too." By this time, I was feeling really confused as to what was going on. What did he mean, "they would have to get rid of her too?"

It wasn't long before two security guards entered the nurse's station and began speaking with the head male nurse. I could hear them talking softly, but I still wasn't able to make out what was being said. That's when I heard one of the guards say, "I'm not going to do it again." His voice got louder, and it sounded like he was becoming agitated. He continued, "I've done it too many times, and I'm not going to do it again!"

There was a short time of arguing, but the voices were mingling together, and I couldn't decipher what they were saying, then the two guards walked out. I didn't understand what was happening. The male nurse, who seemed to be the one in charge, turned to a couple of the other nurses and said, "Now what are we going to do?"

I had no idea what this was all about, and I was already on alert as I had remembered them saying "they would have to get rid of her too," speaking of the attendant from downstairs. What was going on?

It was cold, and I was tired, not to mention, even more confused than before. I was just trying to make some sense of things. I had an IV in my arm and an oxygen tube in my nostrils which made me very uncomfortable. I asked for a warm blanket, and a few minutes later, a nurse returned with one and covered me. The warmth seemed to wrap itself around my body and felt so good that it almost made me forget about what I had just heard.

About thirty minutes had passed, when another security guard came in and the same male nurse that was in charge began talking to him. Once again, they spoke so quietly that I had a hard time hearing exactly what was being said. I assumed they picked up where the male nurse had left off, while speaking with the other two security guards.

All of a sudden, I heard the guard say that he would need eight-hundred dollars in cash before he would finish the job and that it had to be done by five-thirty the next morning.

My mind was racing, trying to interpret what this meant. Were they really planning to kill that female admitting attendant from downstairs? She hadn't done anything wrong! She'd just come up to find out how I was doing. She'd heard that I wasn't doing good and maybe she just wanted to make sure everything was okay. I was feeling extremely anxious as I tried to reason why all this was happening.

Suddenly, my thoughts were interrupted as I heard the security guard say, "Thank you." Then he left. I assumed there had been an exchange, and he'd received the "payoff" to finish the job.

There was a lot of chatter between the nurses in the ICU station throughout the evening. So much of what was being said was in such a quiet tone that I strained, trying desperately to hear what they were saying, but to no avail. I was feeling very uneasy about all I'd just heard.

I was extremely exhausted at this point, yet at the same time I couldn't go to sleep. Too much was on my mind, trying to figure out what was going on. I was aware the nurses were around, but they weren't attentive to my needs. If I needed something, they would fulfill my request, but there was no attention given to me. They weren't even checking my vitals.

Later that evening, I was startled by a loud noise that resembled the sound of a gunshot. My first thought was, "Did someone drop something?" My next thought was a little more frightening. "Was that a firecracker or was it actually a gunshot?" Now, my insides were beginning to quiver. I became anxious, figuring that "the job" they'd been planning against the administrative attendant had just been completed. I went into a panic mode; there was nothing I could do. I could have called out, but "they" were the only ones that would have heard me.

As I lay in my bed unable to move, more questions were coming to mind, like, "Why her?" "Why was it so important that she would have to die?" I had just begun trying to wrap my mind around everything that was going on when I heard the most frightening words ever. "He will have to be gone by then too," meaning, that I would be dead by five-thirty the next morning, along with her.

Now extreme panic set in. I had no idea why they were planning to eliminate me. I hadn't done anything to any of them. I'd never met any of them. Unanswered questions invaded my mind, and the more I thought about everything, an added sensation of dread began to come over me. I could literally feel the fear gripping my body and mind. I felt as if I my body was paralyzed.

It was getting late in the evening, and I should have been going to sleep, but there was no way I could relax enough to fall asleep. I needed to know what had just happened and exactly what they had planned for me. I knew I had to stay awake. I had to be alert so I could hear what they were saying. I lay in that hospital bed, listening to every word that was being spoken in hopes that something would soon be revealed. I needed clarity. My ears were tuned in to everything being said.

Then, I heard the male nurse's voice. I could see him and two female nurses from my bed as they were standing in the hall next to the nurse's station. He was telling the two nurses that there would be calls coming in, and family members would be asking questions about "him," and again, I assumed that meant me. He told them they needed to sound emotionally affected by the event. While he spoke, he kept looking into my room as though he wanted me to know what was going on.

I listened closely, trying to focus with all my mind so I could hear and understand every word he was telling the nurses. I heard him instruct them that as the phone calls began coming in, they were to tell the caller how very sorry they were and that they'd done everything in their power to save "him," but that "he didn't make it." The most death-gripping fear set in. I could feel my body reacting, leaving me with the most helpless feeling I had ever experienced in my life. I couldn't escape their attack because I was trapped by tubing, not to mention, my body was so swollen I could barely move. I was lying in a hospital bed with an IV tube injected into my arm, obviously sedated, and everything was happening so fast I couldn't keep up. My mind was swarming with thoughts!

In just a short time, the first call came through. I could hear the nurse, her voice cracking as though she was going to burst into tears at any moment, telling the person on the other end that I had passed away. She sounded like she really was shaken by what had happened. Just as instructed, she told the caller that my things could be picked up in the morning and that she was very sorry for "her" loss.

I assumed, the nurse had been talking to my wife, Melody, as she had gone home to take care of her mother throughout the night. I knew she would be returning in the morning to check on me and see how I was doing, but that wouldn't be until about nine.

I was just starting to put the last phone call together when I heard the phone ring again. I shuttered, hoping it wasn't another family member. But I heard the same response given to that caller as well.

I instantly got sick to my stomach. My insides were quivering. My mind could only imagine who this might be. I couldn't help it; the tears began to flow as I was envisioning how the family would respond to the news that I had passed away, when in fact I was still alive. How could I get the message to them? I was crying out in my mind. I was becoming frantic. I didn't know what to do! Another call came in and the same rhetoric. Now, who could that one be?

It was early morning by this time, and five-thirty was coming fast. I was totally unaware that my sister, Jill, had been awakened by God and began praying the Word of God over my situation. Her prayers began with Psalms 118:17, but she personalized it. "Bud shall not die but live and declare the works of the Lord." And so, it went with every verse God was giving her. Each personalized to my situation.

I couldn't help but wonder, "How was everything was going to transpire?" Were they going to come in and give me a life-ending medication through my IV, or would they shoot me like they did the administrative attendant? My mind would not allow me to get any sleep. I wondered how the death would take place and how my family would react to the news. This seemed to drag on through the early hours of the morning. I hadn't slept a wink.

Five-thirty finally came, and I was still alive. Why did they let me live? Did someone botch part of the plan? Did they just delay the time for an hour or so? What was going on? My mind was in a whirlwind. I was very worried about Melody and how she was handling all of this. Melody and I were inseparable, and normally, we spent most of our time together. So, to be apart was difficult for both of us.

A new nurse had come into my room after the morning shift-change. I wasn't sure if she was aware of what was happening, so I asked her if she could get my cell phone for me. It was close by, in a bag with all my clothes, but I didn't have the strength to get up. Besides that, I was hooked up to the IV and oxygen and couldn't reach that far. I was shocked and disappointed when she refused, saying that she had other things to do.

Now I was convinced, the word had been passed to all the staff and they were keeping me from contacting my family to alert them. I felt such an urgency to let my family know I was still alive! I had not died! I assumed from phone calls I'd heard that most of them probably thought I was dead.

By now, it was after 8:00 a.m., and I didn't know what to do. I was totally helpless. Melody was sure to be panic-stricken along with all the other members of my family. I had a sister in New Mexico, a brother and sister-in-law in southern Washington, and a sister in Colorado. My son and daughter both lived in Oregon and had been with me at the onset of this ordeal and had gone home. I couldn't contact any of them, and I didn't know what to do.

The time passed slowly, eight-thirty, nine o'clock, nine-thirty, all came and went, and still, no communication with the family. At nine-forty-five, Melody walked through the door of my room.

As I woke into consciousness, the fog began to clear from my head. It was now Sunday morning, January 18. I was unaware that I had just gone through a traumatic event where my lungs, kidneys, and heart had all stopped at the same time. Apparently, I had died and been revived. But now, I was hooked to life support as I couldn't breathe on my own; my kidneys had stopped functioning; and my heart wasn't beating on its own.

I had been in and out of consciousness throughout the day, as the nurses had been in and out of my room, trying to get me to respond. My family had been at my bedside, and apparently, I would only respond to my daughter's voice by opening my eyes as she spoke. But I had no recollection of any of these incidents.

I had begun responding to commands that the nurses were giving me, so everyone was hopeful since I was beginning to show signs that there was brain activity. That night, they started me on kidney dialysis to help with my kidney function, and my lungs were still being drained from the liquid that was continually filling them. My heart, lungs, and kidneys were still requiring the support of machines to function properly.

CHAPTER 11

A New Day Has Dawned

Throughout the night, nurses had been at my side, continuously performing procedures and providing treatments, trying to get my body to respond. But the next morning on Monday, January 19, there was a miraculous turn of events. Just one day after I had died and been brought to life again, we were beginning to witness the miracle God had promised.

Shawna and Gabe spent the night in the family waiting room in ICU, just to make sure they were there in case something happened. It had been a rough night for them with all the commotion of the nurses going on. Neither of them had hardly slept between all the noise and their continuous checking-in on me throughout the night.

When they came into my room the next morning, they were extremely encouraged to find that I'd had a really good night. Melody had also arrived at the hospital by then, and all three of them began to witness something that was nothing short of a miracle.

As the morning progressed, my blood pressure had started coming back on its own. My lungs were needing less support, and my kidneys were starting to produce urine again. I was responding to and following the nurse's commands. As my wife and kids would talk to me, I was able to open my eyes and respond to them. My progress was amazing!

By lunch time, I was able to get out of bed and sit in a chair to eat my lunch. Everyone coming in and out of the room were amazed at what they were seeing! They all commented on how good I looked. It was almost unbelievable!

Shawna and Gabe were so encouraged with my progress that after talking with the doctor and being reassured they could call and get updates, they felt comfortable enough to leave the hospital and head back home.

Just twenty-some hours earlier, I died and was resurrected to life again! My body had been dead for five minutes, and even though I had come back to life, my organs had shut down to the point that they needed machines to keep them functioning. And here we were, right now, witnessing God performing His Word. It was exactly what He said He was going to do! He was doing something miraculous! He was bringing life out of death! The word got out quickly as to what God was doing, and everyone was rejoicing! The prayers continued, and my progress accelerated. To God be the glory!

That evening, the nursing staff said they were planning to move me from the ICU floor onto a regular floor. My healing was coming quickly! Everyone was encouraged and amazed to see God working, as if there was no time to waste. He indeed had a plan. And that plan was only just beginning to unfold. He was about to show Himself in ways that none of us had ever seen.

The next day was Tuesday, January 20, just two days after being revived and placed on life support. My body continued to respond and take over on its own. I had another good night, and my breathing had improved tremendously. This is what everyone had hoped and prayed for, and now, the doctor was considering the removal of the breathing tube. The news just kept getting better! And as the day progressed, so did my health. We were witnessing a true miracle!

It also happened that my memory had begun coming back as well. Up until today, I hadn't remembered anything that had taken place since they moved me from the sixth floor to the second so I could start the chemotherapy treatments. I had encountered two different spiritual visions starting some time on Friday, the nineteenth, and lasting until Sunday morning when I was revived.

Melody came in to visit that morning and I told her, "Boy! You wouldn't believe the things they did to me!" I was referring to the first spiritual vision I had encountered. I thought all the visions had really happened.

Apparently, sometime between Friday night and Sunday, the nurses had to secure bilateral wrist restraints in order to keep my tubes and lines safe. Remember in the vision, I saw the nurse rip the IV tube out of my arm. It must have been at the same time I was the one who was ripping the IV tube out of my arm in the natural realm.

Melody was saying that she saw me trying to get free from the restraints and that I was furious. (If you knew my personality, you would realize how ridiculous and yet scary that must have been.) She said that it actually frightened her to the point she had to leave the room.

That surprised me to hear her version of what happened because in my vision, the mean nurse had ripped the IV from my arm. So, as I began telling her what I had experienced, I was explaining to her what I had seen during my "spiritual encounter." While I was telling her the events, I still believed that what I had gone through was reality.

As Melody listened to my story, she began to realize that I wasn't aware of what *really* happened. She told me that I had been in the same room I was in currently and that I had not been moved. But because of the spiritual battles I had gone through, I argued that I knew what I was talking about and that I would explain it to her when we got home.

At that point, she knew it wasn't worth trying to convince me any differently, so she appeased me and just let it go for another time. As time went on, I would come to understand the difference between what I saw in the spiritual realm and what was actually happening in the natural.

Later that afternoon, Shawna called to check and see how I was doing. She had been keeping pretty close tabs on me since she hadn't been able to come to the hospital. I'm not sure if I was excited or amazed at what was happening, maybe a little of both. As we talked, I was able to share with her all that the medical staff had done for me since our conversation earlier that morning.

Since then, they had removed the oxygen tube because I was able to breathe on my own. And now, I was able to speak with much more ease. They had also removed the kidney machine as I was urinating on my own, and they removed some of the lines going into my neck. My body was still swollen to about four to five times its normal size, but I knew that as fast as things were happening, it wouldn't be long before the swelling would be gone. I was completely off life support! God had performed a miracle!

On Thursday, January 22, only four days after I had died, I was experiencing even more progress. God's healing power was infusing my body. The therapist came in to my room so I could begin my therapy. The first test was to see if I could walk. After everything I had just been through, dying and being revived, my heart and kidneys failing and not being able to breathe on my own, the idea of standing on my feet would be a huge victory. She brought in a walker for me and much to our surprise, not only was I able to stand up, but I walked with the aid of the walker for the first time.

We were so amazed at what was transpiring! Both the therapist and I thought it would be a task for me to walk because it was expected that my legs would be extremely weak, but instead, my legs were really strong. I even tried to run but was immediately stopped by the physical therapist as she was afraid I would fall. Even though my legs were strong, it was a difficult task to walk. They were enormous from the swelling, and I had to move with my legs spread. I knew I still had a long way to go before reaching my complete recovery, but this was sure a better place to begin than what the physical therapist had first thought.

The weekend proved to be a busy one for me as they continued to perform tests. They were constantly tracking my progress and working with me to get stronger. My lungs kept filling up with fluid, so the medical staff had to continuously keep them drained.

All this continued while they were looking for me to transfer out of ICU and into a regular hospital room. It took a while for a room to come available, but the next day, I was finally released from the intensive care unit to another floor. What a blessing!

They had just finished a complete remodeling of that entire hospital floor, and it felt like I'd been transferred to a four-star hotel. In my mind, it could have been because of everything I had just gone through, and the room in ICU. But this room was beyond comfortable, especially for a hospital. Not only was God healing my body, but He had just provided the most beautiful place for the healing of my soul to begin.

Everything had gone so quickly up to this time, I hadn't even had time to process it. Now, God provided a place where I would be so comfortable that I could begin to relax a little. At least between the times of more medical procedures that still had to be done.

By the next day, there were even more advancements as the lymph nodes had started shrinking and the swelling began subsiding. Through this entire process, I had come to learn that lymph nodes, also referred to as lymph glands, were an important part of the immune system. They're located throughout the body but visible only when they're enlarged or swollen. They seem to gather in groups in one area in the body and reflect abnormalities in that area. They can form behind the ears, in the neck, the groin, under the chin, and in the armpits. You and I probably wouldn't even notice that they were swollen, but a doctor would be able to tell through a simple examination.

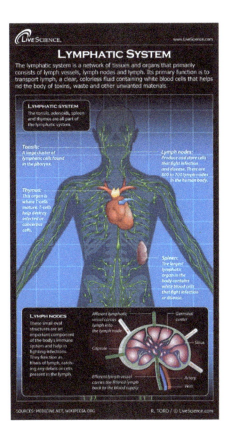

Our bodies have a network of lymph vessels and lymph nodes that are all a part of the body's immune system. This network collects fluid, waste material, and other things, like viruses and bacteria that are in the body tissues outside the bloodstream. Enlarged lymph nodes may feel like pellets under the skin that can be rubbery, often due to lymphoma. They may also be soft and tender, if due to infection, and on their way to forming an abscess.

The enlarged lymph nodes during my cancer attack in 2008 were located in the groin, but the initial pain was felt in my lower back. In early 2015, I felt the attack in my lungs, as I had a very difficult time breathing. I also had bloat that caused shortness of breath.

That was when they determined I needed to have fluids drained from my lungs. When the fluids were tested, it was confirmed that the lymph nodes were cancerous. That's what had been causing the bloat and left me with shortness of breath.

But, while we were finally on the other side, I wasn't completely out of the woods yet as I had so many more procedures that I would have to go through. But by faith, we knew this was just another sign of evidence that God was continually healing my body. All our prayers were being answered, but even greater than that, God was accomplishing His Word in my life. We continued to pray those verses that He spoke in the very beginning. He is the one who spoke it; we just believed it and confessed it and watched His healing power take its effect on my body.

CHAPTER 12

Faith Matters

My father was known as a man of faith. From a child, I watched as my dad would pray for people, and they would be healed. He and my mom loved to go to the homes of people who had recently visited their church. Their hearts were to encourage people in their faith. But many times, during their visits, my dad would learn through their conversation that they were suffering from an ailment.

After sharing Scripture verses on healing, he would ask permission to pray for them and inevitably, as soon he finished his prayer, the person was made well. It happened early on in his walk with the Lord and continued until the day he died. My family grew up with trusting and believing God for healing, and it was just the normal for us.

My youngest sister, Jill, writes concerning the faith of our father:

"As long as I can remember, my dad was known as '*a man of faith.*' I'm not sure if it was because he prayed for people and they were healed, or if it was his trust in God to reach down to humanity and save mankind from an eternity destined for hell, or his simple trust that God would meet his every need. All I know is that his faith touched every person he came in contact with.

"As for me, I witnessed my dad's faith as he would pray for me when I was a little girl. Every time I was sick, I would seek out my dad to pray for me, and more times than not, I would receive healing in my body. It wasn't that we didn't believe in doctors; my dad just believed we needed to go to God first and give Him the opportunity to heal. This continued even into my adulthood.

"His prayers just seemed to touch the throne of God. He prayed faithfully for each member of our family by name every morning. And whenever he heard about a need, he would write it down and faithfully take it to the throne of God until there was an answer.

"In my dad's later years of life, he made several trips to the hospital as his body was getting old and trying to shut down. He recognized these trips as opportunities to share Jesus's love with everyone who attended to him. When he had to go to the hospital, his first thought was, *"Somebody must need to hear about Jesus."* And from that point forward, he sought out the opportunity to share his faith in his Lord Jesus.

"One day, while he was on his deathbed in my home, he seemed a bit unsettled. My sister and I were at his side, trying to comfort him, trying to understand what was troubling him. He started to cry and then he said, *'Who is going to tell them? Who's going to tell them when I'm gone?'* We finally understood what was on his mind. He was concerned for those who needed Jesus and wanted to make sure that somebody was going to carry on where he left off.

"This man of faith, my dad, left the most priceless legacy of faith, not only for his family but for all the lives of the people he touched."

My brother, Bruce, writes concerning the faith of our father.

"It was sometime in 1944 while serving in the Army Air Corp that Dad suffered an incident that formed who he was to become in his later life. When he was somewhere around eighty to eighty-five years old, he began suffering some mental issues and decided to undergo hypnosis. It was at that time he learned that he had been blown out of a foxhole during WWII and a friend of his was killed. He had suppressed this and wasn't aware of the effects it had on him during his lifetime.

"Dad was hard on us kids at times, and I can remember that he had a hard time dealing with family stress. You would always know he was 'gonna blow' when from the side of his mouth he would do a kind of a sucking sound and then, there he went! Poor Jill. Mom always called her Jill the Pill, but I remember her as Jill the Spill. She would always spill a glass of milk or something at the dinner table, you'd hear that sucking sound and then, Dad would blow. Jackie, Bud, and I suffered the same sound many times. The PTSD that he suffered in the Army made him nervous when he encountered stress. I've counted back, and I believe that we moved about twenty times by the time I was eighteen. I asked Dad in his later years why we moved so much. He said he didn't know; he just knew we had to get out, so we moved. Looking back since the hypnosis, he believed it was probably due to the PTSD.

"But Dad had a soft side to him, taking missionaries into our home, working in the church, joining the Gideons, and being a witness to others. He had a missionary's heart as he and Mom were candidates to become missionaries in Papua, New Guinea, with Missionary Aviation Fellowship in 1959. They were declined because of their age, and we ended up moving to New Mexico. It was there that Great-grandma (on Mom's side) conversed with the Lord, and Dad had enough faith to follow the leading that she gave.

"Two years later, we moved to Seattle. Mom and Dad went to work at King's Garden. We had always been given a strong spiritual foundation by attending church (every Sunday, Wednesday, Thursday, youth group) but it was at King's Garden that I believe we, the kids, really saw the dedication that both Mom and Dad had to the Lord. As I look at the four of us, I can see that there is a common spiritual thread that runs through us that bonds us and is directly attributed to Mom and Dad.

"Dad believed in work. We were taught at an early age that we needed to work. We had jobs not only around the house but also paying jobs during our school years. I remember Bud and I wanted to go to football camp and it cost ninety dollars apiece. Dad said we could go, so he lined us up with the next-door neighbor to do yard work so we could earn the money. All four of us kids have a great work ethic, again directly attributed to Dad. There have been times that I have been bitter toward Dad, but as I look back, I am so thankful that he pulled out that spiritual rope on Sunday mornings, tied it to the bumper of the car, and dragged us to church. (I remember praying for red lights so we wouldn't get there so early.) I am so thankful for the breakfast table and hearing Dad reading *Our*

Daily Bread. I am so thankful that he made us read and memorize the Bible. I am so thankful that he and Mom sacrificed so that we could get the education and Biblical foundation at King's Garden.

"I remember Dad telling me in his later years that he felt guilty because he and Mom couldn't really serve in the church because they were "just getting old." So, he and Mom became prayer warriors. They had lists of people that they prayed for faithfully. Dad was funny though; he told me he felt kind of guilty because he couldn't close his eyes during prayer because he needed to read the list. I told him that I thought the Lord probably understood.

"Both Mom and Dad's legacy is that they left us with a strong Biblical foundation, a good work ethic, strong spiritual and family bonds, and showed us to be faithful to the end. For this, I am ever grateful."

My older sister, Jackie, writes concerning the faith of our father.

"Dad *was* a man of faith, that's for sure. There are several things that stand out. Dad would always pray when I had a tummy ache, from the time I was very small and continued into my adult years. He was always there for me. I loved to hear him pray. Those prayers were straight from his heart.

"When our entire family was together, and he prayed, I always cried. His prayers touched me so much! His words were so sweet. There are a lot more memories, but I can't remember them all. I was my daddy's 'little girl' from the time I was born until the day he died. I loved that man so much!"

What do we do, what do you do, when God gives you or me a promise? And more importantly, what do we do when that promise seems delayed in being fulfilled? It doesn't matter if the promise is for healing, as it was in my instance, a rebellious child, a financial matter, or a broken relationship. No matter the promise, it's going to require a pathway of faith.

Where does faith come from? The Bible says, "Faith comes by hearing, and hearing by the Word of God" Romans 10:17. So, where do the promises of God come from? They come from His Word. When God speaks, you can take what He says and *know* He will do what He says He will do. All we have to do is believe.

The most difficult promise to hold on to is the one that has not been fulfilled after having spent many hours in prayer, had others praying for you, claiming God's Word; and after weeks, months, and years, there is still nothing.

We are given so many examples in the Bible of ones who experienced the same thing. Abraham was such a man. God made a promise to Abraham in Genesis 18. And not only did he hear the promise, his wife, Sarah, overheard the conversation concerning the promise. This promise was in regards to them having a son, but its ramifications went way beyond just having a son. The promise was to fulfill a greater purpose.

It wasn't even a new promise, which surely made it even harder to believe. The most difficult promise to take seriously is one that has seemingly and repeatedly not been kept. What kind of promise-maker is harder to believe than the one who has continually not kept their promise?

Sarah did the normal thing that any woman would do at that moment; she began to laugh to herself. She was thinking about the fact that she and Abraham were far beyond the years of getting pregnant. Now, the promise was such an impossibility; it seemed ridiculous.

When she's called out for laughing, Sarah denies having laughed. And the messenger isn't about to let her off the hook! So, he says to her, "Yes, you did!"

Her comment back to him was probably one that anyone of her age would have if told they were going to have child past child-rearing years; she questioned him. "Will I have a child now that I'm old?" She'd been waiting a long time and now it was impossible, except for a miracle from God.

The messenger's retort was, "Is anything too hard for the Lord?"

But Abraham held onto the promise, believing that though this would be a human impossibility, God would somehow come through.

Many times during this discourse, Abraham could have given up. He could have thrown his hands up in the air and cursed God, but he didn't. He kept on the course, no matter what the odds were, no matter what people might be saying, no matter what. God had made a promise, and he knew without a shadow of a doubt that God would come through because God cannot lie.

I wonder, "How would we have done? What would we have done?"

At one point, when Abraham was waiting for the promise to come to pass, he and Sarah came up with their own plan. Perhaps, they pondered, God meant for it to happen this way. And Ishmael was born but not from Sarah's womb.

Sometimes, impatience can be a hindrance, even though we're still believing. Trust God to do what He wants to do, *in His timing*. God was gracious and still had a promise He was going to keep. In the back of Abraham's mind, he knew God would come through. The promised child, Isaac, was born and the Lord did for Abraham and Sarah as He had promised.

God's promises were not just for Abraham but for Sarah too. The Lord's covenant was big enough not just for an old man but for and old woman too. Sarah reaped the benefits of Abraham's faith. Abraham was mentioned as one the Heroes of Faith in Hebrews chapter 11. He had held on to the promise of God, standing on God's promise and didn't waiver.

At the beginning of my hospital stay in mid-January of 2015, how did I know, without any shadow of doubt, that I would not die? When everything said the opposite, how did my family and I have the faith to believe? When doctors were unsure, how were we sure? There were verses from God's Word, promises that we as a family grabbed onto and were not going to give up.

We claimed these promises day and night, praying them back to God and believing He would hear and answer our cries. The only question was, is He going to perform an immediate miracle or was He going to use doctors?

Does God still heal people like He did when Jesus was on earth? If He does, then why do we need doctors and medicine? Shouldn't a strong faith be enough, and isn't that what God wants us to have?

There's no doubt that God intervenes on many occasions to heal people without the aid of medicine, but nowhere does the Bible urge us to reject medical treatment. God has given us the ability to develop modern medical treatments, and we should see them as a gift from His hand. As a matter of fact, Luke, who wrote the books of Luke and Acts, was a physician; Paul referred to him as "our dear friend Luke, the doctor," in Colossians 4:14.

Of course, this doesn't mean we shouldn't pray when someone is sick and ask God to heal them. Ultimately, our lives are in God's hands, and even when He uses medicine to bring about a person's healing, He should still get the praise, honor, and glory. I once heard of a case, where a woman came to a minister for prayer regarding the need for healing. After he anointed her with oil, they both noticed there was no change in her body. It wasn't until four days later that she was suddenly and instantly healed. There are some who heal gradually. We need to leave the how and when to God but *know* His promise is *sure*!

CHAPTER 13

A New Release

It was now Friday, January 23, only five days after being on life support and not having been expected to survive or have any quality of life. But instead, my progress was coming along so quickly that the doctors were already talking of moving me out of ICU and into a rehabilitation program. They were preparing for me to be able to go home!

Just the thought of being able to return home again was overwhelmingly exciting! My stay in the hospital had not been one we'd planned and certainly hadn't come with the idea of dying. So much had taken place in such a short amount of time. It was almost too much to take in.

Melody and I were amazed at how fast paced my recovery was. It was as though I had been placed on a fast track. At least for this part of my journey. We were keenly aware that I still had a long way to go, as there were more chemotherapy treatments in store for me. But for now, the goal was to give me some rehab, make sure I could maneuver with limited help, and then release me to go home. We were so excited! We were finally seeing a little bit of light at the end of the tunnel. But I wanted it to happen *now*!

As I was moved to the new location on the second floor, I was hoping that I would recover quickly enough, that my release would be sooner rather than later. But sometimes, things don't work out as fast as we would like.

Although I was no longer in ICU, my body was still in need of healing before I would be well enough to go home. With all the liquid that kept filling my lungs, along with the drains, I had developed a wheezing. So the nurses gave me a breathing apparatus called a manual incentive spirometer to help clear out my lungs. While using this, it required deep breathing and was actually quite painful. But since I was determined to get well enough so I could go home, I persistently continued the breathing treatments in spite of the discomfort.

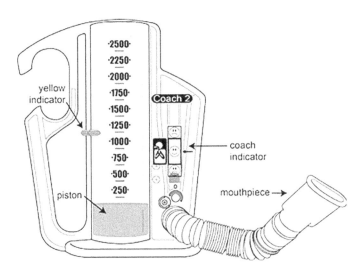

My treatment consisted of breathing air through a tube, which was connected to a large air column containing a ball. With each breath inhaled, the ball inside the column would rise upward and the height it reached was determined by how much air was going into the tube. This was two-fold, as it was not only helping to strengthen my lungs again, but by allowing more oxygen to be released in my body, it was causing me to relax more and help relieve some of the pain.

When I first started using the machine, I found that I wasn't nearly in as good of shape as I had anticipated. The nurses had forewarned me that this would probably be the case but not to get discouraged with the results at the beginning. My lungs had obviously weakened during the time I had died and was placed on a breathing machine to help keep me alive. And just as they thought, while much to my surprise, I failed the test miserably the first few times. I was surprised to see that the ball barely moved.

I was instructed that I had to keep track of my progress each time I performed the exercise by writing down how high the ball moved up the column. That way, both the doctor and I would know how well my lungs were working. I've always been a competitive person, and that worked to my advantage in this case. I kept wanting to see that ball climb higher in that tube so as I continued to breathe deeper, I eventually got the hang of it. And it wasn't long that the ball started rising higher with the breaths, simple things to keep me going so I would keep on improving. It put a little humor on a task that could have otherwise been mundane.

Then there was the other uncomfortable condition of bloat due to the extreme swelling in my body. Because of this, the nurses had to help me move from a sitting position to a standing one, anytime I needed to get up. I hadn't been able to do anything on my own yet, and they had me up and walking to continue building the strength in my legs.

My body had swelled far beyond it's normal size, and honestly, I was enormous from head to toe, almost unrecognizable. My face, nose, mouth, ears, my hands and fingers, feet and toes, every single part of my body was swollen. And with the swelling came much pain, excruciating pain.

Imagine when your fingers swell up as they retain water. If you've ever experienced the pain of what it feels like when they're bumped, you *know* how painful that is. Now, imagine your fingers being *four to five times* their original size because of the water retention. One can't even begin to know what that pain feels like, and my entire body was like that.

I honestly can't describe the pain I felt, as it was horrendous at times; not only from the swelling, but my skin would become so stretched that it would burst open, creating open wounds that would sometimes be three to four inches long. They couldn't sew the skin back together because of the swelling, so they just had to treat my wounds.

I really wanted this part to be over, but until the swelling went down, this was just something I would have to endure. And with every movement, believe me, I *felt* the pain. So having the nurses get me out of bed so I could walk was not a normal procedure. It was painstakingly difficult.

I still had the catheter in me because of all the kidney problems associated with my kidneys being shut down when I died. And the IV was still in my arm. So getting up and moving, within itself, was a very difficult task. The nurse would help me up because of the swelling, but then as I walked, there was the IV pole that had to move with me, along with me holding onto my collection bag from the urine. It was quite the endeavor, and had one been observing, it may have looked a bit comical. On my end of things, not so much. But I knew I had to be persistent if I was ever going to go home.

Everything was now starting to become routine for me. I was doing the breathing treatments and recording them as instructed. The nurses were helping me to get out of bed so we could take my laps around the corridor, and they were still draining the liquid from my lungs. The swelling in my body was even starting to go down ever so slightly. I was also told that I had to start drinking lots of water so they could remove the IV. That was pretty easy since I had been used to drinking in excess of two liters per day prior to this latest adventure.

It was now Sunday, January 25, and they had done a cat scan and a lung tap that morning. The cat scan was to check the lymph nodes to see what they were doing.

We were elated when the results came back, and we heard the wonderful report that they were still shrinking. God's faithfulness had been more than amazing to witness!

The lung tap had been quite extensive, along with being a procedure I had not been particularly fond of. It required that I bend over so that my ribs would be extended apart, while the doctor inserted a needle so as not to touch any part of the bones. The needle had to be carefully and cautiously inserted so that it didn't puncture my lung but would only enter the wall of the lung, as this is where the fluid was gathering. The fluid would be drawn out and then sent to the lab for testing to see if the cancer cells were growing or diminishing.

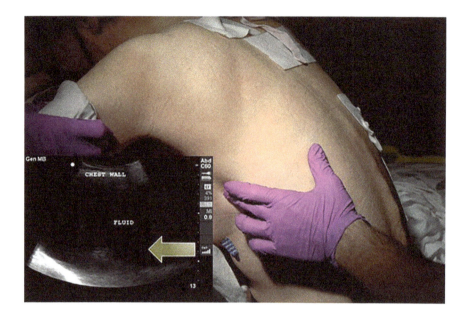

This procedure was also how they drained my lungs. Between the day before and this day, they had drained five pounds of fluid from my lungs.

I was told that the swelling in my body would eventually go down, but for now, it was simply a waiting game. The swelling from so much extra fluid in my body had caused my weight to increase from one hundred and fifty-five pounds to one hundred and eighty-six pounds in just four days. Every day seemed to put me just that much closer to the goal of getting to go home.

The next day, Monday January 26, was monumental. The nurses had been keeping a close eye on my oxygen as it seemed that I was needing it less and less. The day had finally arrived! The oxygen with all the tubes was coming off! It had been so uncomfortable having the tubes in my nose constantly, and I have to say, I was beyond ready for them to be removed. What a blessing that was! All I could say was, "God, You are amazing!" It felt like my life was being given back to me, a piece at a time.

I still needed for my legs to be strong enough before they would release me. So, I had been working really hard at walking the corridor to help in that process. Normally, when the nurse would bring the walker to me, she would walk with me, but today, because I was so determined to go home, I took off by myself. I wasn't only trying to prove to her that I was ready, but I wanted to prove to myself that I could do this. I did good at first, but then my legs began to tire and become weak, so I had to cut my walk short. I took my first lap around the hallway by myself without help. What a good feeling that was!

With each new day, I was making more progress. Surprisingly, the nurse came into my room that same day to inform me that she was there to remove the central line that went into my jugular vein. This was the line that was used to inject medications into my body. Removing the line was a sure sign that I wasn't going to "crash" again and that the doctors were confident of the same. This was a huge step toward my goal of going home, and I knew I had to be getting close, although nobody had given me a day as to when that might take place.

By the next day, I was up and walking again, and this time I was able to finish an entire lap around the west end of the second floor. They also told Melody that she could bring food from home for me to eat. Anyone that's been in the hospital for a while longs for a home-cooked meal, and I was no different. It didn't even matter *what* she brought me. At that point, *everything* sounded good!

One can only imagine the sheer jubilation I felt when the next event happened. The nurse came back into my room and had a big smile on her face. She acted as if she knew something I didn't and couldn't wait to tell me. She held the suspense for just a few minutes, but then she blurted out, "Well, they just told me . . . that . . . they're considering letting you go home as an outpatient!"

Those had been such long-awaited words that I had longed to hear. I almost wanted to cry for joy! I can't tell you the feelings of excitement, hope, and relief that were flooding my emotions. All I could do was look up, and with the most gratitude I think I've ever felt, I kept saying over and over, "Thank You, Jesus . . . Thank You, Jesus!"

I'm not sure if it was because of the excitement of thinking I was going to get to go home, but I was feeling more determination than ever to walk without help. I got the walker and walked an entire lap by myself.

My family called me often as soon as they had received the good news that I was going to be released from the hospital soon. Talking had become much easier since all the medications had been reduced, and I was able to think more clearly. Plus, my breathing had improved so much that I wasn't running out of breath while I was talking. It seemed like each person I spoke with was noticing the difference as well.

It was amazing how, with each phone call, we all praised God as I was able to give so many good reports of what was happening so quickly. The swelling had gone down from where I had just weighed one hundred and eighty-six pounds, and in just a few days, I was already back down to one hundred and fifty-nine pounds. What a testimony it was to the healing power of Jesus, and everyone was marveling at what He was doing! It had just been ten short days!

Now there was only one issue lingering before I could be released to go home for two weeks. There were nine stairs I would have to climb up to the entryway of our home. I had been walking on my own but had not climbed any stairs, and the nurses weren't sure that my legs would be strong enough to accomplish that task.

I was so motivated to be discharged that I told the nurse who was on duty at the time, I didn't think it would be a problem. She immediately led Melody and me to a staircase in the hospital where I was given the opportunity to prove that I was ready for the transition to a home atmosphere. I was going to have to put action to my words. In spite of what she might have thought, I had no doubt that I could do this.

I began by running up the stairs when the nurse immediately told me to just walk the stairs. I so wanted to prove to her and myself that I really did have this. So holding onto the railing, I climbed each stair with ease and strength; I had passed the test with flying colors. Those nine stairs leading up to the entryway at our house would not be an obstacle preventing me from returning home.

I could tell by the looks on both the nurse's and Melody's faces that they were very surprised by what they had just witnessed. As the three of us turned to walk back to my room, Melody spoke with the utmost confidence, "Whoever says that Jesus is not still in the healing business doesn't know Him. The doctors didn't think that Bud would make it, and if he did, he would be living in a nursing home the rest of his life. He also said the swelling in his body would take weeks, if not months, to go away and that was just last week. His swelling is just about gone. Everything is just about back to normal. He has been up walking and climbing stairs, and he is going home today and not to a nursing home! The Bible speaks about healing and prayer! Prayers were going up all over the world for Bud."

I was extremely anxious to leave the confines of the hospital, even though I knew I would soon be returning as an outpatient to continue with the second round of chemotherapy treatments. Melody had already arranged for the time off from work as it was going to require twenty-four/seven assistance for me at home. It took some time to get all the discharge papers together, but the moment finally came when I heard those long-awaited words from the nurse, "Everything's done, and you're ready to go home."

I jubilantly replied, "I don't know what heaven is going to be like, but I think I just experienced a little taste of it."

To say that it was an emotional drive home would be an understatement. While Melody was driving, we could hardly contain our emotions as we shared together all that had transpired in just ten days. Our hearts were overflowing with so much gratitude for all that God had accomplished. And even though I believed God had brought me through this trial for a purpose, I somehow knew that this journey had only begun. I was now ready to take on the task of performing what it took to fulfill His purpose in me.

We were so involved in our conversation that we were surprised to have reached our driveway so quickly. Words could never express what I was feeling at that moment. I sat there for a few minutes with the car door opened; it seemed like the colors had come to life, the air was lighter, and the smells were more vibrant than ever.

As I started to get out of the car, reality hit as I was still having a difficult time maneuvering quickly. I had seen people walking around in the same type of hobbling manner that I had now found myself in. I'd never realized, until this moment, what they were going through. My compassion jumped to a new level of appreciation for whatever it might have been that led them to that place.

It was the most overwhelming feeling of relief as I was seeing the fulfillment of God's spoken word in my life. I looked up at the house and knew I was ready to tackle those stairs, the very thing that once stood as an obstacle to prevent me from coming home.

Melody helped me as I got out of the car, and we walked arm in arm to the stairs. I took hold of the railing with my right hand as Melody held onto my left arm, and together we began climbing the nine stairs to our home. With her support, I made it to top of the stairs and entered the main floor of our home. It felt so good to be home again. The familiar spaces were especially inviting, warm, and friendly. It had only been ten days, but somehow, that time spent in the hospital felt like an eternity in time. Now, with walking through the door of our home, so many memories were returning and with a much more sense of appreciation than ever before. I was finally home . . .

CHAPTER 14

A Much-Needed Break

I was finally released from the hospital on Wednesday, January 28, and knew that I would have to go back to the oncologist in around two weeks, just to check to see how I was doing. But for now, I was home, and the first thing I wanted to do was just go lay on my bed. I'm not sure if I was just feeling tired because of the trip home, or if it was that final letdown of knowing that this part of my journey had been completed. Whatever the reason, I just wanted to lay in my own bed and take a nap.

As I lay my head on the pillow and started to relax, I didn't go right to sleep. My mind was flooded with thoughts of what I had just gone through and the incredible events God had allowed me to go through. What an amazing journey! To God be the glory!

I pondered on a few of the verses that kept me going through the entire ordeal. One was in Psalms 118:17, "I shall not die but live and shall declare the works and recount the illustrious acts of the Lord." Another was in Psalms 118:23–24, "This is from the Lord and is His doings, it is marvelous in our eyes. This is the day which the Lord has brought about; we will rejoice and be glad in it." As I lay there, quietly praying, I soon fell asleep.

Life had returned to a more normal state for Melody and me since I'd been home. Just a couple days after being back, I was spending time with the Lord, praying and reading my Bible, when He led me to yet another promise. It was in Jeremiah 30:17, "'But I will restore you to health and heal your wounds,' declares the Lord." Once again, He was reassuring me that His plan was to restore my health.

I thought I was home to stay, except for the periodical returns to the hospital as an outpatient. My assumption, based on what I had been through in 2008, was that I would go to the hospital for additional chemo treatments but still get to go home right after.

My previous experience allowed me to go in as an outpatient, have my treatment, and return home. Of course, we expected some of the same symptoms as before, such as fatigue and possible nausea. However, I was really hoping and praying this time that I didn't suffer from the depression. The last time, the depression had been more debilitating than all the other symptoms combined. I remembered Melody referring to me as a "shell of a man" during those nine long, dark months until it was over.

On February 3, just six days after being home, I had a follow-up appointment with my oncologist. When she came into the examination room, she was extremely surprised at how good I looked. She told me that considering what I had been through in the past two-and-half weeks, this was not what she expected. I was then able to share with her that it was because of the prayers of family and friends and the healing power of Jesus.

We visited for just a bit while she examined me and then discussed what my next step would be. She explained to Melody and me that I would be scheduled for my second round of chemotherapy treatments sometime in the following week. This would be an outpatient visit, just as originally planned. However, Melody wasn't comfortable with that plan. It was the first chemotherapy treatment that started the whole episode of me dying, and she was not confident that I could go back home without complications. It was a precautionary move on her part, but I believe God had given her wisdom. The doctor agreed that I should be admitted into the hospital for a couple of days while having the treatment for observation.

I knew what to expect. I would have to go back for the second chemo treatment of the six scheduled sessions. The treatment would be expected to take several hours, and a healthcare provider would administer the drugs intravenously, meaning, through a vein in my arm. They would again remind me of the side effects, which could be, but were not limited to irritation around the intravenous site, red or pink urine for a few days, appetite and/or weight changes, indigestion, nausea and vomiting, fatigue, and sleeping difficulties. It could also cause low blood counts and/or anemia, nose bleeds, runny nose, bleeding gums, mouth sores and mouth ulcers, hair loss, skin sensitivity, and nerve problems—just to mention a few.

My appointment for the second round of chemo had been scheduled for February 9. I fully believed that this round would not be quite as eventful as the first. My mindset was that it would be like it was in 2008: have the treatment, leave, go home and deal with some sickness for a couple of days, wait another three weeks and do it again until it was finally over, then resume building a normal life again.

I was admitted in to the hospital on February 9 for my second treatment. They had a room ready for me when I arrived, and once again, I was on the second floor in the same wing as I had been previously. It was very comfortable as I was familiar with some of the nurses on that floor and enjoyed their company. They were all very friendly and accommodating. The first day in my new room consisted of getting vitals and receiving a new IV line in my left arm—all a part of the preparations for the chemotherapy treatment.

When evening came, I took "my friend" (the IV pole) on a walk. The halls were quiet as all the visitors had gone home and most nurses were busy. I strolled through the halls talking to God, and He would answer me in my spirit. We had developed a very special relationship.

My faith began to grow in a new and intense way. I found myself breaking out in the chorus of an old hymn and sang out in an audible voice, "And, He walks with me and He talks with me and He tells me I am His own, and the joy we share as we tarry there, none other, has ever known." As I sang, tears would be streaming down my cheeks. Those very tender moments had become an anchor to our relationship at that time. And as I returned to my room, I felt a warm glow around my heart, a sense of refreshing.

The days at the hospital were uneventful, and everything seemed to go as normal. Thus, it was determined that I could be released to go home. What a relief! So, on February 12, I was discharged. But before I left the hospital, I had experienced the most amazing morning I'd ever had in my life!

As the doctors and nurses came into the room, God used them to open a conversation that led right into my testimony of what God had done for me, in regards to the miracle that He had performed through them.

With other staff, I was able to share the devotion I had read the previous morning out of *Jesus Calling* by Sarah Young. The book was lying on the stand next to my bed, and they would ask me what it was about, which would open the door for me to begin sharing with them regarding Jesus and the church. It was the most amazing situation I have ever encountered. God was filling my mouth with the words He wanted me to say. It wasn't planned out what I would say; I just depended on Him. What a blessed morning!

Later that afternoon, I had shared the blessing in an email with my family. My sister, Jackie, soon responded, "Bud . . . You have taken over where Dad left off! I'm not sure if you know this or not, but when dad was dying and I was there at John and Jill's house, dad was fading in and out. He kept whispering something, and Jill and I asked him what he was saying. He said, 'Who's going to tell them?' Jill and I figured out that he was wanting to know *who* was going to tell *them* about Jesus when he was gone. Well . . . *you* are that one! I wish we could tell him that you have taken over for him and it's all good now. That brings tears to my eyes! You have been *blessed,* Bud! What a legacy Dad left."

As I read those words, I broke in uncontrollable weeping. All I could cry out was, "O God, I'm so unworthy!" It was so humbling to think that God would choose me to carry on the legacy my dad had begun. What an honor and privilege!

It was finally good to be back home again, and unlike the previous return home, I felt like I was doing much better and would be able to return to my normal activities even sooner. Melody drove me home from the hospital, and it hadn't taken long before I realized I wasn't quite as strong as I had anticipated. With the aid of a cane on one side and Melody on the other, we once again made our way up the nine stairs to our house. By the time I got into the house, it had taken every ounce of energy I had, and it was all I could do just to get to the couch so I could rest.

In the next couple of days, I could only go part way from the living room to the back of the house before I was out of breath, and my legs were so weak they were giving out on me. Fortunately, my mother-in-law, who lived in the bottom level apartment of our home and who my wife cared for, had a spare walker. So I was able to use that to get around and began building muscle and stamina again. Within a short period of time, I had built up enough strength that I was able to walk up and down the stairs without help.

I was beginning to feel really good with each new day and felt like my energy level was increasing. I was tired of just sitting in the house, so one day, I decided to help Melody out in the yard. We were pulling weeds, and I was bending down to reach them and pull them out. I actually hated yard work, so it was out of the ordinary for me to enjoy pulling weeds. I was pretty proud of my new-found activities, and so I was eager to share it with my doctor, only to find out that working on the ground was dangerous for me as my immune system was very low.

At the same time, Melody was not only a full-time caregiver to her mother and now, me, but she also took care of our grandkids. The doctor informed us that, that, too, would have to be changed as it wasn't good for me to be in close proximity to the grandkids. Since children are more apt to carry germs and, thus, spreading them, it could make me more susceptible to sickness. We were having to adapt to this new lifestyle, one activity at a time. We were finding that because of my compromised immune system, there was a lot more I couldn't do than what I could do. And now, I had to include interspersed rest into my daily routine.

I was soon to find that the rest was not only good for my body, but during that downtime, God would begin healing my soul as well. It was while I was resting that I would pray and seek the Lord. Sometimes, it was times of thanksgiving, while others would consist of finding understanding and purpose for what I had gone through.

It was during one of those times of thanking the Lord for His faithfulness to me that I had a thought. I had been reflecting back on the time when I had died and been brought back to life. I had completely forgotten that two years earlier, during one of my visits to the VA hospital, I had to fill out a living will. One of the decisions Melody and I had to make together at that time was whether or not I wanted to be resuscitated if I were to die. We made the decision and agreed that in the living will, it would be stated that I would *not* be brought back to life if I passed away.

That form had been filed with the VA two years prior, and at the time I died, they didn't have time to go look to see if I had a DNR on file, so they brought me back to life. And it wasn't as if I had come back to life right away; it took five minutes after I had died! God had to have brought that back to my remembrance, making my resurrection from the dead even more providential. He *wanted* me to live!

There was another day as I was pondering the spiritual attacks I had experienced at the hospital and as I was talking to the Lord about it. I had this thought, "I wonder if the spiritual battle I went through at the hospital was the breaking of the curse that had been placed on me by the Navajo woman in New Mexico."

While I had this thought in the hospital and knew the curse had been broken, suddenly, I was realizing that it had to have been the victory over the grave that broke the curse. And then to see how the Lord used it as a witness to His faithfulness and power was awe-inspiring! I had come through this fearless! I was experiencing a new-found boldness as I shared my experience with others, with no hesitation or intimidation!

God was truly bringing restoration, not only to my physical body, but He was restoring my soul. I was reminded of David's prayer in Psalms 23, "The Lord is my shepherd, I lack nothing. He makes me lie down in green pastures, he leads me beside quiet waters, he refreshes my soul. He guides me along the right paths for his name's sake. Even though I walk through the darkest valley, I will fear no evil, for you are with me, your rod and your staff, they comfort me. You prepare a table before me in the presence of my enemies. You anoint my head with oil; my cup overflows. Surely your goodness and love will follow me all the days of my life, and I will dwell in the house of the Lord forever."

Restoration was happening in both my body and my soul.

CHAPTER 15

God is Relentless Too

Soon after my chemotherapy treatment, Jill and I were talking. She shared that right after I'd had that terrible vision, where I thought I was going to be eliminated by some of the hospital staff, she'd had a thought. As she looked back to what the Lord had revealed to her in the vision of the Navajo woman, she realized that the curse was against the firstborn son and was a curse of death. When she had first heard "curse of death," she told me about it, and now she was beginning to understand what I had gone through.

As we continued the conversation, we began realizing that the "curse of death" had followed me all throughout my life. It had affected churches I pastored, ministries I'd been involved in, relationships, finances, business ventures, and more. I had experienced "death" in almost everything I had put my hands to.

Now that the curse had finally been broken, I was seeing that curse reversed. Even though there was still a battle involved, God was bringing me victory with every step I was taking. Was it easy? Not in the least! Would I have chosen a different path had I been given the choice? Indeed, I would have! But I was placed on this path, and God was giving me the grace to walk it with Him.

So many times, after we've been in a spiritual battle and seen the victory, we let our guard down. We don't understand that we may have won the battle, but the war is not yet over. Satan probably isn't finished. Sometimes he may not return for an extended length of time, while other times he goes from one attack to another, seemingly as not to give us a break.

The story of Job in the Old Testament always comes to mind when I think about spiritual battles. An unusual scene had taken place, where Satan had appeared in heaven before God. He asked Satan, "Where have you been?"

Satan replied, "I've been going to and from the earth and walking up and down it."

The next question is somewhat interesting as He asks Satan, "Have you considered my servant, Job, that there's none like him on the earth? He's a blameless and upright man, one who fears Me and abstains and resists evil."

Satan smugly replies to God's comment, "Are you kidding me? He doesn't fear You for nothing. Look at what You've done for Job. You've basically hedged him in with all the protection he could ever want and poured out prosperity and happiness on him so that everything he puts his hand to, increases. Why wouldn't he put his trust in You? I challenge You to take away all he has and watch him curse You to Your face!"

This gets even more interesting, as now, God takes the challenge, but seemingly at Job's expense. He tells Satan, "Take notice all that Job has, all of his possessions are now in your power, but you cannot touch Job himself."

Satan left the presence of the Lord, and the next thing we hear is unbelievable! One day, Job's sons and daughters had gathered at his eldest son's home in celebration of his birthday and were enjoying the festivities.

A messenger came to Job and said, "The Sabeans (men of stature and rivals of Israel) just came and took away all your animals and have killed all your servants with swords, and I was the only one that escaped to tell you."

And while he was still speaking about this catastrophic event, another messenger came and said, "Lightning has fallen from the skies and burned up all the sheep and the servants, consuming them, and I was the only one that escaped to tell you."

Again, as he was speaking about this tragedy, there came another messenger, saying, "The Chaldeans divided themselves into three bands and made a raid upon the camels and have taken them away, and they killed all the servants with swords. I'm the only one that escaped to tell you."

Yet, while he was speaking about all the bad things he had just witnessed, there came another message, bearing even more devastating news, "Your sons and daughters were eating and drinking wine in their eldest brother's home when a great whirlwind from the desert came and knocked down the house, so it fell on all of them and killed them. They are all dead, and I was the only one that escaped to tell you."

We're then told that Job tore his clothes, shaved his head, and fell down on the ground and worshipped the Lord, saying, "Naked and without possessions, I came into this world from my mother's womb and naked, without possessions, I will depart. The Lord has given, and the Lord has taken away. Blessed be the name of the Lord!"

In this, Job sinned not nor charged God foolishly. What a blow to the devil! I can't even imagine, receiving even one of those reports, let alone all of them, and definitely not all at once. I don't know what I would do. Job lost all his animals, sheep, and camels. Animals were the representation of wealth and all of it was gone in an instance, everything he owned. But not only the animals were gone, all his servants had been killed, another sign of wealth, completely annihilated. And now, if things couldn't get any worse, Job receives word that all his children had been killed by a possible tornado. Were there grandchildren involved? I have to wonder even though it's not mentioned.

From what it sounds like to me, Job was left with his home and his wife. His bank account had been wiped out, his occupation severed, and all his offspring, those meant to carry on his legacy, were dead. He was left with nothing, and yet, he did not curse God as Satan accused he would do if this were to happen.

Satan had just been allowed to attack all Job's possessions, and when the test was over, Job remained faithful to His Lord. His afflictions began from the hatred and jealousy of Satan with the Lord's permission for wise and holy purposes. There is an evil enemy of God, who is continually seeking to distress, to lead astray, and if possible, to destroy those who love God. I'm reminded in John 10:10, "The thief comes only to steal and kill and destroy. I came that that they may have life and have it in abundance."

While we are on this earth, we are within Satan's reach and his plans have always been to destroy us. Why does he hate us so much? The answer is because he hates and is jealous of God. He wanted God's position in the beginning and rebelled against Him, taking a third of the angels with him. Who is this demonic army that we contend with today? They are the enemies of God, Satan and the fallen angels, who now take orders to accomplish Satan's wishes and desires. Desires of destruction.

But the good news is, we have One greater! "Greater is He who lives in you, than he who lives in this world" 1 John 4:4.

The battle is real, but we have One that has already defeated the enemy. "And having disarmed the powers and authorities, He made a public spectacle of them, triumphing over them by the cross" Colossians 2:15.

And we have been given all the weapons of warfare to defeat the enemy. "The weapons we fight with are not the weapons of the world. On the contrary, they have the divine power to demolish strongholds. We demolish arguments and every pretension that sets itself up against the knowledge of God, and we take captive every thought to make it obedient to Christ" 2 Corinthians 2:4–5.

It has become evident to me that God doesn't quit either. It isn't that He strong-arms us until we surrender to Him, whether it's with His sole intent to draw us to salvation or as a believer, to draw us into a closer relationship with Him. He will not force His will upon us.

At times, we might feel anger at His wooing. We may even feel anger toward Him, as if to say, "I'm through with you, God." The thoughts may enter our minds, "If He was so all-powerful and all-loving, why doesn't He make things better? Why don't I have more money? Others around me are living for the devil, and they're doing better than I am. They have more money, nicer things, and they're healthy, and yet, You allow me to be attacked. I'm through with trying to live a Godly life."

Even David, who was a man after God's own heart, cried out to Father God and said, "These are the ungodly people, who always prosper and are at ease in the world; they are the ones that have increased in wealth." In other words, "What's the use?"

Here is the good news. God won't let us go, no matter what. Thoughts may race through our minds, saying, "What kind of God are you? I don't love you. I'm even having a difficult time believing in you. I just want you out of my life! Why won't you let me alone? Even when I want to get away from you, you won't let me go."

That is when we learn that God is a relentless God. He wants each one of us to choose to love and follow Him. He wants us to become like His Son, Jesus Christ. It is called spiritual growth. Years ago, this process was spoken of as sanctification, meaning that God slowly molds us into the likeness of Jesus Christ by setting us aside, shaping us, affirming us, and even rebuking us. We used words such as *holiness*, but today, we prefer terms like growth and spiritual maturity.

Some of us have envisioned spiritual maturity as continuous acts of self-cleansing. We seemingly feel like we have to keep on embracing rituals and behaving in specific ways to make ourselves good enough for divine acceptance, especially by doing more and more and more. If we pray more, serve more, give more, or add more charitable service to our overly crowded lives, we *might* make ourselves good enough. Thus, we become holy or more spiritual in our own minds.

Instead of thinking of the Christian life as what we do, isn't it time to emphasize once again what God does? That's really the biblical perspective; Scripture provides hundreds of examples of God breaking into human existence, chasing us, wooing us, reaching out toward us, embracing us, and changing us. Why won't God let us go? Why does He allow bad things into our lives? The answer is because He love us so much, He is never willing to stop. He won't let us go.

Even when we may feel very alone in this world, we should rest in the assurance that God pursues us. In fact, He loves us so much that He gave the most precious gift of all time. He sacrificed His Only Son, a man who never, ever sinned, though He was fully man, He is fully God. Because He did not sin, He did not owe the same wage of sin that every other human owes. Yet, Jesus willingly gave His life on the cross as a ransom for our own. He paid that debt that He did not owe. Once we believe what Jesus did for us and make it personal, no matter how far away we fall from Him, God still loves us and pursues us.

As long as we live in this sinful and fallen world, we will sin and as believers, although we no longer owe that sin debt because Jesus paid it all, we may still have to deal with the consequence of sin. Yet, God pursues us, teaching us the effects of sin on our life. He *never* gives up on us. He *never* lets us go. All because He loves us and because He is faithful.

Satan pursues us in an unrelenting manner for his evil purposes, while God persistently, out of love, attends to our growth unto Christ-likeness.

Everything I was going through, even though I had never anticipated such things happening to me, was all a part of God's bigger plan for my life. He chooses the best paths for us, and while we don't always understand, we learn to follow and trust Him. It's when we get to the end of our trial that we can look back and say, "Truly, You were in this, Lord, and now I understand. It was good for me." But until then, we're asked to simply believe and follow. That's where I found myself in this part of my journey.

It was now March 3, and once again, Melody and I were making our way to the hospital for my third round of chemotherapy. It was the same procedures all over again, as they prepped me for the treatments. Sadly enough, it had become such a common event that it just seemed like the same old routine for me. The entire procedure would soon be completed, but at least this time, I got to go home right afterward.

Everything had gone really well and without complications, but the next day, I was starting to feel the side effects of the treatment. I was experiencing some dizziness and was a bit weak, but the good news was I wasn't nauseous and didn't have the chills and sweats this time. The first few days after the treatment were always the roughest, and with the last round, I had been in the hospital, where everything had been monitored, making it a bit easier. So far, I was encouraged to see that the symptoms were pretty mild.

I was getting back into my daily routine and feeling good again, when I got a call from the VA. It had only been nine days since my last treatment, and I knew it would be about three weeks before another was due. So I felt a little apprehension as to why they were contacting me. They called to inform me that I needed to come in for a consultation regarding a bone marrow transplant. I have to admit, I had a sinking feeling in the pit of my stomach. It felt like I had just been hit again! This had come out of left field and was totally unexpected; it felt like another attack from the enemy!

CHAPTER 16

Knocked Down but Not Defeated

It seems like Satan tends to side-swipe us to surprise us and to disrupt what we thought God was going to do at a certain time. This was going to be one of those times. But I shouldn't have been surprised because this is just the kind of thing Satan does.

It's quite interesting because looking at the life of Job again, he had just made it through a terrible ordeal and now, he was about to start round two. While the first round was an attack against Job's possessions, round two was going to attack Job's physical body. Pain in our bodies is sometimes the most difficult attacks to deal with as sometimes the attack can last for months or even years.

Once again, the same scenario from his previous visit is replayed. Satan presented himself before the Lord and was asked where he had come from and his answer was the same, "From going to and from the earth and walking up and down on it.

And just like before, the Lord asked him, "Have you considered my servant Job? There is no one on earth like him. He is blameless and upright, a man who fears God and shuns evil. And he still maintains his integrity though you incited me against him to ruin him without any reason."

Satan responds with a smug, "Sure, any man will give up his possessions, but put forth Your hand and touch his flesh and bones and you will see that he will curse You to Your face."

And once again, the Lord replied, "Go ahead, he's in your hands, but do not take his life."

So Satan left the presence of God and tore into Job. Terrible sores from head to toe were inflicted upon Job, so much so that Job took a broken piece of broken pottery and began to scrape the sores. The ancients were accustomed to show their grief by significant external actions, and nothing could more strongly denote the greatness of the calamity than for a man of wealth, honor, and distinction, to sit down in the ashes, to take a piece of broken earthen-ware and begin to scrape his bare body to try to remove the painful sores.

By this time, even Job's wife had had enough. With her tone being a bit harsh, she exclaimed, "Do you still hold fast to your blameless uprightness? Renounce God and die!" They had already lost all their positions and their children and now Job's health was in question. His wife was done!

But even in all this, Job's reply was, "You're talking like a foolish woman! What do you think? That we should only accept the good things that comes from God's hand and not accept misfortune that comes from evil?" In all this, Job did not sin with his lips.

My point is, Satan doesn't give up! The encouraging news is, even though we all go through some suffering in our lives, whether physical, financial, relationships, spiritual, or whatever, we can know that God is still in control, and He is always there. He loves and cares for us. He may not necessarily remove the difficulties that we face, but He will bless us as we have need and finally glorify us, promising that if we remain faithful until death we will receive the crown of life.

In my case, it was now round two with the bad news of a potential bone marrow transplant. After reading the article on the Patient Care and Health Information by the Mayo Clinic on the internet, which stated, "A bone marrow transplant poses many risks of complications, some potentially fatal," I was really torn as to what I should do. The risk could depend on many factors, including the type of disease or condition, the type of transplant, and the age and health of the person receiving the transplant. It went on to state, "Your doctor can explain your risk of complications from a bone marrow transplant. Together you can weigh the risks and benefits to decide whether a bone marrow transplant is right for you."

To be honest, that didn't sound too encouraging to me. I knew I would have to pray with Melody concerning what to do, as it seemed pretty serious, and I really needed to know the mind of the Lord as to what to do. Together, we sought the prayers of family members and friends to know exactly what He wanted us to do in this, as neither Melody nor I, knew which direction we should go. God had given us a miracle two months ago, and I knew His will would be accomplished as long as we followed. I just wasn't sure what His will was at this point.

While Melody and I were still praying about what to do, we had a second consultation on March 17. They assured us that the diffuse large B-Cell lymphoma would return sooner or later with a vengeance, and that they strongly suggested I go ahead with the bone marrow transplant.

At that same time, they were concerned that the cancer may have entered my spinal cord. So once again, there were more tests involved. If there was cancer in my spine, it had the potential of moving up to my brain and cause tumor growth. I was scheduled to have a PT Scan and a CT scan in two days so the doctors could see exactly what was going on. The advantage of PET scan over CT scan was that it would detect developing diseases at an early stage, unlike in the CT scan.

In addition, I also needed to go in for an MRI, which was not my favorite thing to do. The procedure would be an extensive test lasting two hours. And worse than that, I would have a mask put over my face making me look like "Freddy Krueger" in the "Nightmare on Elm Street" film series. The MRI would be scheduled for some time the next week.

In the meantime, I would need to come back to the hospital for five days so they could administer my fourth chemotherapy treatment. He mentioned that this one would be much more extreme than the previous ones. This one would go through my system and even attack the cancerous fluids that had gone into my spine.

Melody and I were still contemplating whether or not to go through with the more invasive bone marrow transplant, when we were scheduled for a meeting with the stem cell collection team. The doctor wanted to make sure we knew exactly what to expect, taking into consideration my general physical condition, diagnosis, stage of disease, and treatments that I had previously gone through.

There would be a number of tests performed to make sure that I was healthy enough to undergo the procedure.

Given that the risks could be serious, deciding whether to get a stem cell transplant for cancer treatment was not an easy decision. So to ensure that we felt more at ease, they let us know that the decision was not the hospital or the doctors but ours alone. At that time, we still needed more information as to what some of the risks might be before we could make the decision to move forward.

We were informed that some of the risks that could apply to me were relapse, where the cancer comes back, or organ damage, new secondary cancers, abnormal growth of lymph tissues, hormone changes in the thyroid or pituitary gland, and cataracts, which would cloud the lens of the eye, possibly causing vision loss. So, this was *not* an easy decision.

However, the benefit I would receive, included replenishment of the body with healthy cells and bone marrow. Following a successful transplant, the bone marrow would start to produce new blood cells. The new blood cells, in turn, had the potential to attack and destroy any cancer cells that survived the initial treatment.

With the new information, Melody and I talked and prayed about what we should do. And after weighing the pros and cons, we decided that I needed to keep moving forward to the completion of the transplant process. We wrapped up the appointment with signing all the paperwork and were ready to begin.

Next, they would begin preparing for a stem cell collection. The good news was that by collecting my cells, instead of using a donor, it would shorten my recovery time substantially. Over the next couple of months, they would be collecting and freezing my stem cells, and then I would have to wait another month. During that month, I would receive another chemotherapy treatment along with radiation, and finally, I would be ready for the bone marrow transplant.

The stem cell collection sounded pretty easy as I had so many blood draws by this time, one more I thought, wouldn't be a big deal. Following that I would have a couple of weeks to go home while they were running my blood through their machines and collecting the stem cells. The end result, if successful, would be that the cancer cells would be gone.

Since Melody and I had prayed about the bone marrow transplant and felt I needed to go through with it, this all seemed good to us. Although at the time, we were a little skeptical and we didn't have a clue as to what was to follow. The promise that I would get to go home for a couple of weeks was very inciting and seemed to cloud my mind on all the pieces in between. After all, they had told us there would be times that would be brutal and a very difficult series of procedures. Again, all I could think of was I was going to get to go home in between treatments.

On March 23, I went in for what I thought was going to be a consultation regarding the PET scan and cat scan results from the week before. But instead, when I arrived at the hospital, I was informed they were going to be performing a spinal tap, taking fluid from my spinal cord and putting chemo into my spine.

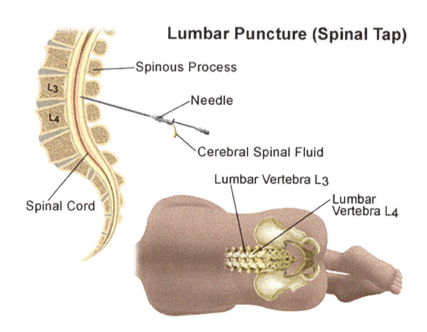

Melody went with me as she wanted to know how the spinal tap or lumbar puncture was performed. The nurse led us to a private sterile room with a hospital bed, where I was prepped for the procedure. I had to lie still in a fetal position because opening the pressures couldn't be reached accurately if I was sitting upright.

Once they located the proper place to insert the needle, a mark was made on my skin to note the exact place to make a puncture. The area was then cleaned and injected with lidocaine to numb the area. Within a few seconds, the spinal needle was injected, and another one was placed inside that needle, and the fluid was extracted.

A small amount of chemotherapy solution was forced up through the needle into the spine and up into my brain cavity, within a timeframe of around twenty to thirty minutes. Then the fluids were extracted and were sent to the lab to be tested for cancer. At times, it was painful but for the most part, I was comfortable and relaxed. It wasn't long before the procedure had been completed, and I was feeling relieved that it hadn't been nearly as scary as it had sounded.

The test results came back positive for cancer, and now, I would have to come back to the hospital every Monday and Thursday for chemotherapy treatments, as the cancer had spread into my spine. This would take place until the cancer had been cured. Along with that, I would be admitted into the hospital tomorrow for the five-day stay so they could perform the fourth of six chemotherapy treatments on the lymphoma, and every twenty-one days after that, until they were completed.

I was admitted into the hospital next day, where I was given a twenty-four-hour drip for the chemotherapy and had been scheduled for the MRI during that stay. I wasn't looking forward to the MRI at all, but the long-dreaded day finally arrived. I'm not typically claustrophobic, but after entering that big tube and having a suffocating mask placed over my face, I entered a new-found fear. Questions began to flood my mind such as, "What if the electricity goes out?" Or, "What if the guy out there forgets about me?" Or "What if I suffocate in here?" It's amazing how fast the mind can come up with negative thoughts. It's also amazing how slow time can move when one is placed in such an uncomfortable position.

It wasn't long after the seemingly, time in eternity I spent in that tunnel that a nurse from the second floor came and got me, and I rode in a wheel chair back to my room. I got situated in my bed, and the doctor came in and gave me a run down on my next steps.

I was released on March 28 to go back home. It had only been four days instead of the five, and I was very thankful that I hadn't had to stay another day. It felt like I had spent so much time at the hospital that being home was uncommon. I could hardly wait to get there: my own bed, Melody's cooking. I could hardly wait! The last treatment had been pretty brutal, and I was feeling very weak, but I was feeling strong in my spirit! I knew the Lord was still in the healing business, and I couldn't help but praise Him for His goodness.

The next morning when I woke up, I was feeling extremely dizzy and had thrown up twice. So, Melody took me back to the ER at the VA hospital so I could be checked out. We weren't taking any chances! Come to find out, when I had been released the day before, they had failed to give me a fluid refill, which meant I was dehydrated. After an easy two-liter hydration, Melody and I were on our way back home again.

On March 30, I had my third spinal tap, and everything went very smooth. On my first spinal tap, the cancer count had been really high, three hundred and ninety-six, and by the second tap, the count had dropped down to forty. They figured this tap should be around four, and by their estimate, the next one should be zero. I would need one more to confirm it and then two follow-ups to kill any stragglers.

I was feeling really good about the cancer count report, but when they told me the results from my MRI, I thought I was going to jump through the roof with excitement! The MRI had shown "no abnormalities" (their word for cancer) in my legs or my head. That meant there was no cancer in my brain! I was praising the Lord all the way home from that hospital visit. God had been so faithful, and we were seeing His complete healing taking effect!

Throughout the week, I hadn't been feeling very good, but I figured it was probably from all the chemo treatments. My appetite had decreased, so I wasn't eating very much either. On Saturday morning, April 4, I decided to take a drive to Puyallup, thinking that maybe the drive would do me some good. But I got extremely tired along the way and had to cut the trip short to return home. During the drive, I became so dizzy and confused I had to pull over to the side of the road and recuperate.

On Monday the sixth, I was admitted back into the hospital due to having a fever and the chills. On Tuesday, they discovered I had an infection and put me on antibiotics. By Wednesday, I was having nosebleeds that that they had a hard time stopping due to my immune system not being strong enough to fight it. I was declining quickly, and nobody could figure out why.

That Wednesday, my oncologist made a visit to my room to talk about the cancer and the treatments and to see how I was doing. I could tell that the oncologist didn't have the same belief in God as me just by the way he was talking. We visited for a few minutes, and I answered some of his questions about how things were going. Then he casually looked over and noticed a book on the stand beside my bed. It was my devotional called *Jesus Calling*. He asked me if that was my book, and I acknowledged that it was. The doctor followed by saying, "So you are . . .," and he paused for a brief moment, so I finished his sentence by saying, "I am a devout follower of Christ."

He didn't respond with anything, so I continued, "You know this was a miracle, don't you?" I went on to explain, "You know how I know it was a miracle? God told me, and He told my wife and He told my sister two weeks before anything happened that there was going to be a miracle. We didn't know what kind of miracle He was talking about. Then He told my wife there was going to be two miracles. And on the day I died, He told my sister that I was not going to die, but I was going to live."

Apparently, that last thing I said caught his attention because he finally responded and asked, "How did she know that?"

I replied, "Through the Bible. That morning, she was reading the Bible, and all the verses were about living and not dying. There were many verses. But one of them said, 'I shall not die but live, and shall declare the works and recount the illustrious acts of the Lord.'"

The look on his face was in total amazement! Then the oncologist explained something that had happened, of which we had no idea, "You didn't die just once, Bud. You died twice. We brought you back to life once, and then you died again, and we brought you back to life a second time."

I had goose bumps all over my body! If one time of having died and been revived wasn't already enough, God brought me back the second time with a resurrection! After just a short pause because I was trying to process all this, I said, "This was a miracle, and nobody can tell me any different!"

The oncologist replied, "I can't say that it's not, and I wouldn't."

That just confirmed what the Lord had laid on Melody's heart that there would be two miracles. I died twice! I knew I had experienced a Divine Appointment that day. This was unlike any Divine Appointment than I had ever encountered.

My time in the hospital had started to take its toll on my body as I developed bed sores, had some nose bleeds, and developed severe constipation. And things were about to get even worse. Yet, through it all, I still had joy and peace in my heart. Psalms 28:7, "The Lord is my strength and my shield. I trust Him with all my heart. He helps me, and my heart is filled with joy. I burst out in songs of thanksgiving." And in John 16:33, "I have told you these things, so that in Me you may have peace. In this world you will have trouble. But take heart! I have overcome the world." Only the Lord can provide these things for us if we will allow Him the opportunity. He doesn't promise a life without trials, but He does provide His grace to go through them.

I was going to need His grace more than ever in the days to come.

CHAPTER 17

Not Out of the Woods

My unexpected hospital stay was being extended. How I longed to be at home, but my body just wasn't strong enough, and my immune system wasn't fighting for me like it should. I'd had a platelet treatment because my blood was not clotting, and we were hoping it would begin to start working soon since I was having so many uncontrollable nosebleeds. And I was scheduled to have another MRI due to suffering with extreme dizziness, and they weren't sure if something was adversely affecting my brain.

It was now the eighth day of my hospital stay with no hope of being discharged anytime soon. And as if things couldn't get any worse, I had now contracted a type of bacteria in my stomach called clostridium, which affects the heart and eyes. It also had the potential of causing sepsis, which could be life-threatening. Sepsis is when the body responds to infection in a negative manner and causes injury to its own tissues and organs. And considering I'd already suffered from cardiac arrest, the doctors were *very* concerned.

They had given me two blood transfusions and tried several different medications to try and eradicate the bacteria, but none of them worked to kill it. It seemed like every day they were putting a new medication through my PICC line via the IV.

This had gone on for an entire week when the doctors finally told Melody they couldn't locate the infection. They had been frantically trying to find the origin of the infection so they would know exactly which bacteria they were attempting to eliminate. I also had a severe inflammatory response to the bacteria. Melody observed that I was getting weaker and weaker every day, and the doctors told her that if they couldn't locate and treat it soon, I would die. This was an extremely serious matter, and the doctors were starting to panic.

The original PICC line to my heart had to be checked for bacteria and then was replaced with a much less invasive peripheral line. Next, an ultrasound was performed to see if the bacteria had caused any damage to my heart. Once again, we received another good report that there were no abnormalities found in my heart, although the search for the bacteria was still on.

The bacteria had finally been located in my blood, which enabled them to treat it with the proper medication. There was such a sense of relief, especially among the medical team, as time was running out and my body was quickly declining. There had been so many people praying God would give the medical staff wisdom in this entire process, and we were now experiencing the fulfillment of their petitions.

Within a couple of days, I had already begun to feel the effects in my body of the antibiotics doing their job. I can't describe how good it felt to feel good again! I was regaining strength, and finally by April 21, fifteen days after I had been admitted into the hospital, the infection was gone!

I was about to hear the sweetest words ever, as the nurse came into my room and announced, "It looks like we'll be discharging you tomorrow!"

That same familiar sense of relief came over me again. Home had become a precious privilege, not something I took for granted anymore. I would still have to return to the hospital to receive antibiotics treatments every day for a short while, plus, they were going to remove the PICC line from my heart. A Port would then be placed into my chest for the next phase of collecting my stem cells in preparation of the bone marrow transplant.

But for today, I was just looking forward to getting back home and not being hooked up to all the tubes. The thoughts of being able to move around without any restrictions, enjoying Melody's home-cooked meals again, and sitting outside, taking in the fresh fragrances of spring, all seemed heavenly. Tomorrow couldn't get here soon enough!

The next day, the doctor stopped in to see me before I was discharged and as we chatted for a few minutes, I told him, "I am so happy that I'm getting better. You do know that a miracle is about to happen." I believed it with all my heart!

I was finally home! I felt quite weak, which was to be expected, but I was confident that day by day, the Lord would help me to get stronger. The gratitude I was feeling at that moment for all the prayers of so many people was overwhelming. Looking back and reflecting on everything that had just happened, as there were some pretty intense moments during my two-and-a-half-weeks stay in the hospital, I was more than amazed. Even though the doctors told Melody there were some real touch-and-go times where they were very concerned for me, yet just like so many times before, God had been so good and proven His faithfulness.

I had to go back to the hospital the next day for a chemical cleanse and to get another dose of antibiotics. Fortunately, it was on an outpatient basis, which meant I got to go back home as soon as the procedures were completed. For the chemical cleanse, they used nebulizers to detoxify my lungs. But while I was there, I learned that they had also planned for my first bone marrow draw. This was the part of the entire ordeal I was dreading. This meant they were starting the first stages of my bone marrow transplant.

I had been back and forth to the hospital the last five days in a row to finish my antibiotic treatments for the previous blood infection and was so glad that today, I was going to get to stay home. There were no more appointments now until tomorrow, when I would begin the first heavy-duty chemotherapy treatment, but even then, I was going to get to come home. Melody had arranged to take a ten-day leave from work since the treatment would require that I had twenty-four/seven care *at home.*

Melody and I went in to the hospital early in the morning, Thursday, April 30. The first heavy chemo treatment had been administered, but once again, my body reacted to the chemotherapy and put me in another tailspin. My body was extremely weak, and I was feeling sick and disoriented. I had entered into a mental state of confusion, and when the nurse asked me what the date was, I told her it was January 13. Then she asked me who the President of the United States was, and I responded, "Ronald Reagan." At this point, they knew something was very wrong and decided to admit me into the hospital. Once again, I would not be going home.

Once my family got word of what had happened, they began to call. First was my daughter, Shawna. I tried to talk to her, but I couldn't understand what she was saying, and my speech was slurred due to all the medication. I kept asking her to repeat herself, and finally, we just ended the conversation because I couldn't make any sense of what she was asking me.

The next day, I was feeling extremely lethargic, when my brother Bruce called. Normally, he and I laugh and joke when we talk, but this time, I really didn't feel like talking. He had expressed his concern that I might be feeling depressed, but I pushed it off to just feeling bored. He encouraged me by saying how much he respected me for my obedience to God's plan in all this, and with that, he said he would keep in touch and we hung up.

I'm not sure if I was even aware at that time of how I was feeling; things were fuzzy, and I was having a difficult time staying mentally focused. My family became very concerned and began getting the word out that everyone needed to be praying. It seemed like just when things started to improve, another battle began to knock me down. This battle was different as it was attacking my mind.

When it was just my body being attacked, I could remain focused on the Lord and that directly affected my attitude in keeping things on a positive note. But with the mental confusion, I hadn't been able to fight against it. So, God brought in prayer warriors to begin interceding on my behalf.

On May 4, the doctors were beginning to think that the blood infection had returned and began drawing blood to see what was going on. I was still very weak and having difficulty in getting my words out when having to speak. My mind was slow in comprehension, so I had to really think about what words I needed to say.

Thirteen days after having had that first heavy-duty chemo treatment, I was still in the hospital. I had been running a fever, and now they thought it was because my white blood cell count was increasing. It seemed like there was a lot of guess-work involved with each new symptom I was developing, a kind of hit-and-miss approach at times. But I was finally starting to comeback mentally.

The diagnosis for what I had just gone through was another bacterial infection. My immune system had been so compromised that my body didn't have the ability to fight off any germs. Unfortunately, this would be something we would have to contend with for quite some time.

I was still in the hospital on May 18 when it was time to begin removing the stem cells. They were able to use my own stem cells as opposed to using a donor's, which would aid in making the healing time quicker. This procedure would have to be done at the Seattle Care Alliance, so they would transfer us from the hospital via a taxi service. It sounded easy enough, but after taking a long while for the taxi to come and pick us up and by the time we got to Seattle Care Alliance, we were just ready for this whole thing to be done.

They got us set up in the room so I could be prepped and had Melody sit close by, where she could observe. As the nurse began, she explained to us that the stem cells were immature cells from the bone marrow that turned into mature red blood cells, white blood cells, or platelets. Next, the stem cells were collected from my blood using a machine that separates the blood through a centrifuge. My stem cells were collected into a bag and the rest of my blood was returned to my body.

The procedure had been quite extensive, and Melody was intrigued by the way they had withdrawn the blood, then removed the stem cells, and returned the blood to my body. The nurse had taken the time throughout the procedure to explain what she was doing each step of the way.

When the stem cell removal had been completed, they thought they had collected all the stem cells they needed from this one procedure. So we waited, and finally the word came back. They had only been able to collect about half of what they needed, and I would have to return the next day to finish retrieving the remainder of the cells. We returned to the hospital, and I settled back into my room.

The following day, Melody came back to the hospital. We walked down to the entrance of the hospital to catch the taxi that would take us to Seattle Care Alliance, where again, I would have more stem cells removed. We waited and waited and no taxi, just like the day before. We waited so long that we were afraid we were going to miss our appointment. So we finally ended up calling the Bone Marrow Transplant Department, and they were able to locate a taxi to come and pick us up.

We were confident that the rest of the stem cells needed would be collected on that day, and we were looking forward to all of this being behind us. Again, we went through the same technique of withdrawing the stem cells and were assured that there was a ninety-nine percent chance that this would finish up the collection. But later that day, word came back that we would have to return once again the next day as they hadn't been able to collect enough.

This was, by far, the lowest day I'd had since being in the hospital. I was promised that when they finished collecting the cells, I would get to go home for two weeks, while the stem cells were being frozen and prepared for reinsertion. I am normally a very easy-going person and not one that gets angry easily, if ever at all, *but I was very upset*.

That night, after Melody had gone home, my frustration flared up more and more as the minutes lingered on. Finally, I'd had enough. I pushed the call button and the nurse on duty came into my room. I told her I wanted her to call the doctor because I needed to speak with him. She gave me the strangest look and informed me he was at home. And with even more frustration, I explained to her that I didn't care, I wanted to speak to him *now*. He had told me that I would be able to go home.

The nurse had him call me, and as I spoke to him, my frustration came out in full force as I told him I was done, and I was going home. He listened as I vented, and once I had finished, He told me that I *could* go home and that I had every right to do so. He continued, and I could hear the compassion in his tone as he tried to reason with me. His soft tone helped me to calm down enough so I could listen to what he had to say. He began explaining that we were only a tiny way from completing the collection and that if it wasn't finished the next day, I could go home, and they would figure another way to complete this. By that time, my emotional outburst had turned into quiet reasoning, so I agreed to complete the process.

CHAPTER 18

Blessings in a Crisis

The next morning felt like a brand-new day. My attitude had changed drastically from what it had been just twelve hours earlier. Melody and I had climbed into the taxi for the third straight day and headed for Seattle Care Alliance. Upon our arrival, we were met by a very friendly, courteous staff as usual and were immediately directed to the small room where they would extract the remaining stem cells.

As we were getting settled in, the nurses offered to bring us some snacks and drinks to make us a bit more comfortable as the procedure would take the usual six hours. The normal prep was done, and soon the procedure began. Melody was still very curious as to the mechanics of the process and enjoyed watching the blood come out of my body and run through the machine. There was a television in the room, creating a very casual atmosphere as well as to help make the time go faster.

That afternoon, while the nurse was charting some of the information needed, we began to talk. Melody had stepped out of the room for a short while to grab a snack. So I started telling the nurse that this whole event with the cancer, dying, and coming back to life had been nothing short of a miracle from God. As I continued to tell her the many things that had transpired, I then shared that it had been God-ordained. At that point, she became even more interested and asked, "How did you *know* it was God ordained? I want to know more."

I began sharing with her where my experience started, when God spoke to me of how much He loved me and that He would never harm me, and of the miracle He promised. She was even more intrigued by now but just continued to listen quietly as the story continued. I went on to explain all the incidents briefly, that my lungs had filled with fluid which led to my trip to the ER, and that leading them to finding the cancer. I also mentioned the chemo treatments, and then how things started going downhill very quickly.

When I got to the part of the story where I died and was brought back to life again, not once but twice and being dead for five minutes, she gasped! "Wait a minute! You died more than once? I mean, you died, twice? How in the world are you here right now, talking to me? How did this happen?"

I explained to her that my sister awoke at five-thirty that same morning, and God led her to several verses in the Bible, all about living and not dying, and that she began to pray those prayers before I had even died and without even knowing what was happening. And then I told her of the hundreds of people that had been praying for me when I had gone into the ER. I also shared that without God, I wouldn't even be here right now and shared my experience of knowing Jesus as my Savior.

At that, she began to cry and said, "I need that same experience in my life."

It was at that time I shared with her that what Jesus had done for me, He would do for her. At that moment, she prayed and asked Jesus to forgive her of everything she had ever done and asked Him to come into her heart and take over. Her prayer was so sincere as she confessed how much she needed Him and wanted Him to be her Savior. Her words were spoken as she wept, and I could hear the relief in her voice.

After regaining her composure, she told me that she was so glad I had come back for a third day as that was going to be her last day. She would be transferring to another hospital. Now, I was awe-struck! I had to tell her that I almost didn't. So I shared my experience with her about the evening before and my conversation with the doctor, that God had used him to get me to come back. By that time, we were both crying! We knew we had just experienced a Divine Appointment!

I hate to think what might have happened if I had not been obedient and gone back for that third treatment. I had no idea that it was God who had planned this; I just saw it as an inconvenience to me.

We've all, no doubt, experienced those "what if" times in our lives. It may have been insignificant for some, while life changing for others. What if I would have gone home when I was so frustrated at the length of time it was taking to finish this procedure? What if I would have gotten my way and gone home, where it would have been much more comfortable? What if I wouldn't have been obedient to the Lord as He was directing this whole scenario?

It has happened throughout the ages. There's a story in the Bible that speaks of a man with leprosy who knelt down in front of Jesus and pleaded with Jesus to heal him. In that day and age, people with leprosy had to be isolated from other people, not even being able to live with their families. They had communities set up outside the towns just for lepers because it was so contagious. Yet, the man begged Jesus, "Please, please, heal me. If you want to do it, I know you can."

Jesus felt compassion for the poor man and touched him. No one ever touched a leper since it was so highly contagious and easily spread from one person to another. But as soon as Jesus touched the man, He said, "It is my desire to heal you. Be healed!" The man was healed immediately, and the leprosy was completely gone.

So Jesus sent him to see a priest, which was required during those times. When someone was healed, they had to show themselves to a priest to prove that they were well. The priest would then officially state that they could go back and live with other people. Jesus *warned* him, "Make sure that you don't tell anyone about this healing. But go and show yourself to the priest and offer the sacrifices that Moses commanded for your cleansing as a testimony to them," which was the law at that time.

This was done as confirmation that the healing was real. Instead, the man left and talked to people freely, spreading the news, just as Jesus told him not to do. As a result, Jesus could no longer enter a town openly but stayed outside in lonely places.

What if? What if the man would have obeyed? What might have happened? Would there have been many more people who would have been healed in that area? As a result of this man's disobedience, we're told that Jesus could not enter a town *openly* anymore but had to stay outside of the city.

So many times, we think we know what's best, only to find out that we probably should have made a different choice. Sadly, sometimes we disobey the clear teaching or leading of the Lord because we think we know a better way, but other times, we just act, instead of asking God what His will is. By doing this, our attempts at doing good end up hindering His will. He wants us to obey him even when we can't understand the reasons behind what He's asking us to do.

The man's disobedience, though well-intended, interfered with Jesus's desire to fulfill his mission. In the same way, our disobedience to the Lord today often interferes with His desire to accomplish His mission through us.

The tears, acceptance, and gratitude of the nurse made it evident to me and many others that God had given me a divine appointment, even though I had not been happy about having to go back a third time.

That day on May 26, they were able to collect enough stem cells, and the stem cell removal process was finally over. And just as the doctor promised, I was discharged and free to go home.

As I awoke the next morning in my own bed, in my own home, I had the most overwhelming feeling of relief. I was loving every moment of being home and everything it included: waking up that morning and going to bed that night, knowing Melody was with me. I had come to appreciate so many things that before, I had just taken for granted. I couldn't thank the Lord enough for all He'd brought me through.

CHAPTER 19

We're Almost There

The next month would prove to be an extremely busy one, as preparations were being made for the bone marrow transplant. And Melody and I were learning quickly that this was going to be a step-by step, process.

I was feeling really good again, between enjoying the comforts of my own home and having the freedom to come and go as I wished. And along with my appetite coming back, I was feeling a little bit stronger every day. The Lord had walked this journey with me and I was confident that He would continue to watch over and care for me, as I began taking all the necessary steps in preparing for the transplant.

As Melody and I proceeded with the radiation and chemotherapy consultation, we were able to glean so much information in understanding the procedures I was about to go through. Both treatments were necessary in killing everything in the bone marrow, both good and bad. Which in turn would allow the stem cells that had been collected to be inserted and, ultimately, overtake anything in the clean bone marrow and begin growing *healthy* bone marrow. The procedures would more than likely make me sick and very weak until the new stem cells produced healthier cells. The time frame we were looking at for recovery was around six months.

Melody and I both felt good about the information we had learned and, once again, put our complete faith and trust in the Lord, knowing that He already knew how things were going to go and had it all planned out. He was a loving Father that would not bring me harm, as He had promised in the beginning.

The next step was a trip to the radiation clinic where they measured my bones for the radiation treatments to begin the next week. The schedule would consist of eight treatments within a four-day period and last for one and a half hours per day. These treatments would leave me nauseated and weak, but I was supposed to remain as active as possible even throughout the fatigue. I could also expect sores in my mouth and throat but would have medication to help with that if necessary. The greatest concern was that there could be no fevers over one hundred degrees, as that could show signs of infection, and at that point, I would have to get to the hospital immediately. Once again, I was trusting the Lord to get me through the next few weeks. I had come this far with the Lord's help and knew this would all be wrapped up through His might and power.

During the next trip to the VA and meeting with my doctor, Melody and I were given the schedule of all the treatments for the next month. Instead of being an outpatient, they were going to admit me into the hospital for twenty-one days. Upon hearing that, Melody and I immediately looked at each other, knowing what the other was thinking . . . here we go again. It was so difficult when I was in the hospital for Melody's already busy schedule. But we both knew God was in control, and He must have a better plan in my staying in the hospital, so we didn't argue the point.

I would be admitted in just four short days, which would be on Monday, June 8. During my stay in the hospital, I would be receiving the radiation treatments, my sixth and last round of chemo, and then an infusion of my stem cells. These would prove to be excruciating times.

We had thoroughly enjoyed the next few days at home, especially knowing that it was going to be at least three more weeks until it would happen again. And the planned three weeks were not guaranteed, as we had discovered in times past, it could be even longer. Over the weekend, Melody and I had planned to make my time at the hospital, as much like the comforts of our own home as we could.

Upon admission Monday, June 8, I was given a private room in the Bone Marrow Transplant Unit that came furnished with a television, a comfortable bed, my own bathroom, a chair, and a table.

All the basics of making it seem more like home. Of course, it still felt like a hospital room with all the medical equipment and smells of being sterile and free of germs, but with Melody's help, we were going to make it *feel* like home.

When I awoke the next morning, I received the usual routine check of the nurse coming in to take my vitals, ate breakfast, and took the meds provided for me. I also met with the doctor working in my particular unit. Depending on Melody's time schedule, I would get ready for a shower, which was not my favorite activity of the day. The shower room was always very cold, so I would enter the shower room, turn on the hot water to get some steam going, and heat up the little space. Then after about ten minutes, I would get my clean clothes ready and get into the shower.

That pretty much became my daily routine, providing me with some sense of normalcy. Many times, when Melody would come to visit, we would lay together on my twin size bed and hold hands or cuddle up to each other and watch television together. This became our new normal from the time I entered the Bone Marrow Unit.

Throughout my stay, Melody would arrive shortly after the doctors left the room, with a laundry basket full of my clothing from home. She would then take the time to sort the clothing by sweat pants, t-shirts, sweatshirts, and underwear and place them in an orderly fashion on the window sill of my room.

Every other day, she would take my dirty laundry, walk it down to the car, and return it in two days as clean clothes, carrying the laundry basket back through the halls of the hospital and up to my room. I always viewed this as a sacrifice of possible humiliation from others as she did this. I've never seen such compassion from a caregiver in a hospital. It's no wonder why I called her my "angel."

From this moment on, I was dressed in sweats and tennis shoes, rather than wearing a hospital gown, making it feel more like I was at home. Early on in my stay, Melody continued to make it more comfortable for me and surprised me with thoughtful little gifts. One day, she brought me a poster board, loaded with pictures. She had taken one of our wedding pictures and attached it to the board, along with pictures of her and me throughout our marriage. I was amazed at the thoughtfulness she had put into the making of the collage, especially when I noticed that she had chosen a picture of her and I when we were in high school; we were high school sweethearts. The picture was a black-and-white photo that we had taken in one of those twenty-five cent booths when I was sixteen and she was fifteen. This was such a special picture and had always been one of our favorites.

The first sight I would see when waking up in the mornings was the warmth and sweetness of that montage. Then Melody would walk through the door. I could hardly wait for that moment, each and every morning. We would walk down the hall so I could build up my strength, holding hands and walking together, and talking with one another, allowing us to continually stay on the same page.

The next two months were destined to be intense compared to the last four. From that point forward, the treatments would begin: radiation, chemo, and the insertion of the stem cells. I was well on my way to the beginning of the end for this part of my journey.

I was soon going through the procedure of having my PICC line replaced with a Hickman line that would serve as the host for receiving chemotherapy, medications and for blood withdrawals. This would make it much easier for me and the nurses as the procedures would become common occurrences.

Next, there were the eight sessions of radiation treatments required, two per day for four consecutive days. They consisted of full body scans that took forty minutes each and required that I stand still for twenty minutes scanning one side of my body, then turning around and standing still for another twenty minutes. It was very boring but necessary, so took that as an opportunity to spend the time praying for my family. I prayed for each member: my wife, son, daughter, sisters, brother, and all their children and grandchildren. I found that if I prayed, the time went by faster.

Following the radiation treatments, the worst began to happen. After each treatment, as I would go back to my room, the ease with which things were first transpiring, started changing quickly. I began to lose weight, and my strength was noticeably diminishing. While I had been warned that these symptoms were very possible, I was still hoping for a better ride. With each new day of treatments, I was finding it more and more difficult to force myself to get out of bed and walk.

It was within a very short time of receiving the radiation that I was diagnosed with neutropenia, which meant I had an unusually low number of white blood cells in my immune system. Anyone who entered my room was required to wear a gown and a mask, so as not to spread any germs. The white blood cells were much needed as they attacked the bacteria and other organisms that would try to invade my body. These cells that were created by the new bone marrow would travel through my bloodstream, moving to any areas of infection where they would consume and then neutralize the offending bacteria. It was of utmost importance at that time to watch for a fever, infection, bacteria, viruses, yeast, or other fungi.

I was highly susceptible to infection, anywhere in my body, because of the radiation treatments. If once the infection started, it had the potential of spreading throughout my body and causing a fever, cough or sore throat, diarrhea, a headache or sinus pain, a stiff or sore neck, skin rash, and sores in my mouth or on the tongue. I had already experienced several of these symptoms during the days following my last chemotherapy and radiation treatments and was fully aware that any of these symptoms could occur at any time and without notice.

It was a miserable time of pain and frustration as the treatments had started, and I had been experiencing a loss of appetite, which led to my losing weight. I tried forcing myself to eat, only to result in becoming nauseated and throwing up. I lost five pounds in one week and was increasingly growing weaker and weaker, which made me very lethargic. I also began feeling disoriented, in which I was finding it difficult in navigating my way to the restroom.

I was so prone to infection at the same time. Melody not only wore a gown, she was required to wash her hands before entering the room. Since she worked in a children's daycare and the kids always had some kind of sniffles, fever, or some "bug" that they picked up from another child, she had the potential of bringing one of those "bugs" into my room; it could cause some really big problems for me. My room had to remain an absolute hygienic environment during those times.

It was now day four in the hospital. The radiation treatments had been successfully completed, and the next step was to start the aggressive chemotherapy treatments. I was encouraged because right after the first chemo treatment, the only symptom I was having was dizziness, but that was all soon to change as well.

Melody brought in some home-cooked food, thinking that I may have a better chance of enjoying eating a home-cooked meal rather than the hospital food, but only after one bite, I knew it wasn't the food that was the problem. Nothing tasted good anymore, and I was feeling really bad that I couldn't even eat my own wife's cooking which I normally loved.

The feeling of fatigue worsened and just getting out of bed had become laborious. I knew I couldn't continue to lie in bed and let this thing destroy me, so I forced myself to get up and walk. Having been made aware of several patients in the same transplant unit who had stayed in bed and three of them dying, it had become a motivating factor in my intense drive to be as active as I could.

The doctors and nurses became very concerned with how much weight I had lost and did their best to work with me on a diet plan, even bringing in a nutritionist, but it was an uphill struggle. I was given Boost, a high-protein drink, which wasn't too bad, and I needed the energy, but even those were getting challenging to swallow.

Not only did I not have appetite, but now I had huge silver-dollar-sized sores surfacing in my mouth. My tongue was raw, and my throat had developed the same lesions. I couldn't swallow and was being fed nutritionally and given fluids all through an intravenous line. The sores were very painful and lasted for two weeks before I could swallow water or any soft foods. I was given pain medication to help, but it wasn't working either, making the pain almost unbearable. Speaking had become just about impossible as it hurt so bad to talk, so I quit trying to converse. Family members would call to talk, and at first, I tried, but I just couldn't do it. I felt bad, but the pain was so intense I had to opt out.

They started inserting my stem cells during this time as well, and I was receiving three bags of my cleaned cells per day in three separate sessions. It was also during that time I started showing signs of a fever, so the antibiotics were increased to help prevent another infection. I was experiencing bloody noses and spitting up blood, but the medical staff kept reassuring me that everything happening to my body was all common side effects from the treatments I had, and that I *would soon* find relief as they would begin to diminish. I just couldn't wait for that time to begin!

It had now been twelve days into my hospital stay and was June 20. Although everything was going very fast in the completion of my treatments, it seemed like it had been forever since I had been home. As the days passed, my desire to return home increased, all the while the side effects from my treatments were diminishing, just as the doctors and nurses said they would.

Nine days later, on June 29, I had experienced tremendous improvement! The sores in my mouth had lessened to the point that I was able to put my false teeth in, and my appetite had started coming back again, so I was able to eat breakfast that morning and had successfully kept it down. Melody and I had continued our walks through the halls, and even when she wasn't there, I would take the walks by myself.

Well, I say by myself, but the Lord was with me. As I was healing, the Lord led me to visit some of the other patients on the floor during my walks. I prayed with some, and with others, I shared my testimony of the miraculous things God had done in my life in the last six months. What I found during those walks and talking with the people is that God had provided me with a mission field right there in the hospital. It was to help and encourage others who were facing the same things I had just gone through.

Many times, we get to minister to others, not knowing whatever happened with them. Everyone in that unit had cancer, and in the back of their minds was the thought of dying. I wanted to give them hope—the hope of Jesus—that whether they lived or died, Jesus would be there with them each and every step of the way. It gave purpose to my stay in the hospital and made it easier to complete my journey there until it was time to return home again, and we were almost there.

CHAPTER 20

In Honor of the Caregiver

One of the most important but often forgotten people involved in an extended trauma situation is the caregiver. Yet, without the caregiver, so many people living in impossible situations of caring for themselves would be left on their own to live out a quality of life, leading to neglectful circumstances.

Most often, a caregiver may be a partner, family member, or close friend who have no professional training but only a deep love for the person whom they are caring for. And may not understand that *their own* physical, emotional, and mental health is vital, while helping with the person in need. So many times, since they are the lifeline of that person, they bear the weight of carrying the one they love, emotionally and physically, which eventually can lead to periods of stress, anxiety, depression, and frustration.

There are times, they will try to shrug it off and just keep going, feeling that they are weak or uncaring for having such emotions. The caregiver feels so much responsibility for their loved one's well-being that they are willing to sacrifice their own feelings for that one.

At times, it can seem overwhelming as the care is constant and demanding, depending on the needs of their loved one. There is such a feeling of compassion and concern for their loved one's comfort that eventually, if not given a break from their responsibilities, they will reach sheer exhaustion. Even in this, they may begin to feel guilt for not feeling qualified to carry out their inherited tasks.

The trips to the emergency room that last well into the morning hours and not having been prepared leaves the caregiver drained, emotionally and physically. Since, they've not slept all night or had anything to eat or drink, the mental state of the caregiver begins to decline. Now, comes the decision, whether they should leave their loved one in the care of the hospital staff or stay and continue taking on the responsibility of caring for the loved one themselves. The guilt of leaving is temporarily dealt with when the caregiver decides they need some rest and goes home.

But when the caregiver gets home, they began to see all the things that still need to be done at home, so instead of resting, they pick up where they left off before going to the emergency room the day before. So much for the much-needed rest. If they're lucky, they may get in a short nap before returning to the hospital. But still, their emotions are constantly being tugged at by guilt, feeling they need to be in two places at once, when finally, they just give in to whatever the highest priority is in the moment.

Not only does the caregiver sacrifice but so does the rest of their family. The time required for the care of their loved one takes precious time from the other members of their family. And even though they may understand, the caregiver still feels the burden and guilt for not being able to be enough for everyone.

There are times in a caregiver's life that they are living in survival mode, going from one crisis to another, that if they are not given a break, they will themselves end up breaking. When this happens, it can easily lead to a physical or emotional breakdown. Then the guilt of not being able to handle it sets in all over again.

When the caregiver reaches this point, they feel like it is an impossible task for them to continue on and begins to reach out for other alternative solutions. It feels like a relief in the beginning of the search, until they begin having thoughts that they just failed what they were entrusted to complete. What a vicious cycle it becomes.

So, once again, after the "self-talk" of "you can do this" or "you can't give up now" or any other myriads of "why you need to keep moving forward," the caregiver begins where they left off, continuing the care for their loved one. They feel like they have no other choice.

All of the above examples of feelings are real for a caregiver. That is the world they live in and the worst part of it is nobody else knows it or understands. They get the pat on the back, or the acknowledgement of all their hard work or a genuine thank you, and deep down inside, they are appreciative of the compliments, but it doesn't bring any relief to the caregiver in their situation.

When it comes down to it, caregivers really are the unforgotten helpers, and without them, many loved ones would be left alone. Personally, I don't even know how to thank a caregiver because there are not enough thank-yous out there to express the gratitude every one of you deserves.

So, this chapter is meant to honor each and every one of you, and I ask that God rewards you for every minute that you have given, sacrificially and unselfishly, putting another's needs before your own. I pray abounding blessings upon you along with peace, comfort, rest, courage, and grace.

I am reminded of the scripture in Proverbs 19:17, "He who is gracious and lends a hand to the poor lends to the Lord, and He will repay him for his good deed." (The word *poor* in this verse represents one who is in a lowly or weak place and needing help.)

No one could ever repay you for the sacrifices you have made. There's no way that anyone could ever understand all that you have given. And even though you have given freely and you wouldn't have had it any other way, your unselfish dedication has not gone unseen by the One to whom it matters the most. His promises are true, so get ready! Your reward is great as He promises to "repay you for your good deeds."

As I entered the hospital in the middle of January 2015, my precious wife, Melody, was already a caregiver for her elderly mother who had been diagnosed with serious dementia. Her mom was not only affected mentally, but she had hearing difficulties, couldn't walk, and was legally blind. She had a motorized scooter, which helped but made it difficult for Melody because her mom couldn't really see things in detail and at times would run into furniture or walls.

In a typical day, Melody would wake up and begin caring for her mother around 6:00 a.m. She fixed her breakfast and took it down stairs to the apartment, where her mom lived. The apartment had one bedroom, a bathroom, a kitchenette, a storage room, and a front living area. While her mom was eating breakfast, Melody would go into the bedroom and set out the clothes her mom would wear that day. Before helping her mom get dressed, Melody would make sure she took her pills and then a sponge bath was administered as her mom wasn't able to get into a tub or a shower. Every weekend, she would wash her mom's hair and then set it in curlers.

Melody tended to her mother's every need, until another caregiver would arrive to relieve her. At that time, she had to drive to our daughter's house, get three of our grandkids ready for school, and then drop them off at their respective school and daycare. As soon as they were safely at school, Melody would drive to work where she would take care of small children from nine o'clock in the morning until two o'clock in the afternoon.

Following her work schedule that required the constant care of small children for five hours, she would drive to the VA hospital and spend two hours as a caretaker for me, then drive back home again to cook dinner for her mom and make sure that she was fed. Then she would get her ready and into bed for the night. On top of that exhausting schedule, Melody would be called, many nights, to attend to her mother regarding a variety of needs that her mom required.

At the same time, she also had taken on the responsibilities of our financial dealings including paying the bills as it was usually one of my duties in the house. She also kept up the yard maintenance and all of her own household chores, like cleaning, grocery shopping, and cooking, just to mention a few.

There was also the responsibility of being the property manager for her mother's five-bedroom rental where five college students lived. Rent was late many months, and then there were times of bickering that Melody ended up having to referee.

If that wasn't enough, Melody did the laundry for all of us, took her mom to doctor appointments, and chauffeured her mom around when she got bored and wanted to get out of the house.

For the person not involved in helping another as a caregiver, it is easy to overlook exactly what is involved. It is a very demanding job and requires much patience. The caregiver has to be cheery and wear a smile on their face at all times. This is beyond difficult at times because their mood will generally affect the ones they're taking care of. It's refreshing to get a heartfelt thank you from time to time.

Melody received an email toward the end of my time in the hospital from my sister, Jill, which read, "I just wanted to thank you for all of the updates on Bud but especially for being there with him every step of this journey. We have all been concerned about him, and rightfully so, but sometimes the caregiver goes unnoticed. And that person goes through just as much, if not more, during the critical times. Bud has said over and over how much he loves and appreciates you being there with him. He looks so forward to your time together. That means a lot to me and the rest of our family. I know this has been very difficult for you too. I just wanted you to know how much I love and appreciate you and all that you have done and are still doing for him."

So many times, while I was in the hospital, I heard the nurses say it is the caregiver that makes the difference in how a patient respond to treatment. I knew they had noticed and were talking about the "angel" in my life, my wife, Melody. Only the Lord can repay you for all you've done, not only for me, but for your entire family. I love you with all my heart.

CHAPTER 21

Welcome Home

How do you feel when you stand on the verge of reaching a long-awaited goal? Are you happy, sad, or relieved that the journey is nearly over? Are you frightened of the tests and trials that still lie ahead, or do you view your future with courage and faith in God?

Let's visit the story of Job one more time. As we think back on everything that happened to him in such a short amount of time, we only begin to realize that this was just the beginning of a long journey ahead of him. He had lost all of his wealth, his children, and his good health. Never in his life had he suffered any kind of loss, as he was a blessed man. That is, until Satan took notice. It was there that the testing and trials began.

Not only had he lost everything, but his wife and friends turned against him. His friends accused him of being sinful and deserving what he was experiencing. What an awful time for Job. We're not told how long Job's sufferings lasted, but imagine if it had gone on for a month, two months, a year, or even five years.

But I don't want to give the impression that the story ends here, with just knowing about his sufferings, although they were more than I could ever imagine. There was a purpose in all of that Job went through, even though while he was going through the trials, he had no understanding of any purpose. Yet, he never turned his back on God. He questioned Him, but he never rebelled against Him through his entire ordeal.

However, we *are* given a clue to what God may have been trying to do when Job is questioned by his friends about his righteousness. Job defends himself by saying he's not lustful toward women;

he's never committed adultery; he's always lent to the poor; he's not greedy; he's always treated other people with respect; he's not an idolater; and on and on, he went, justifying his righteousness.

But when the last friend out of four had listened, he was disgusted at Job's defense because he was righteous in his own eyes, justifying himself rather than God. And even though some of the things he said to Job were accurate, God was still not pleased with the friend's actions.

Finally, we come to the end of Job's story after his friends had inaccurately judged him in his situation, and God appears on the scene. In order to save time of reading four chapters' worth of questions, I will just summarize it with a few quotes from the scripture itself to give a small glimpse into what God was trying to accomplish.

Job 38:1–5, "Then the Lord spoke to Job out of the storm. He said: 'Who is this that obscures my plans with words without knowledge? Brace yourself like a man; I will question you, and you shall answer me. Where were you when I laid the earth's foundation? Tell me, if you understand. Who marked off its dimensions? Surely you know!'"

And God continues to speak like this for two entire chapters, each verse questioning Job. Then God stops for a moment and speaks to Job for the second time.

Job 40:1–10, "The Lord said to Job: 'Will the one who contends with the Almighty correct him? Let him who accuses God answer him!'

"Then Job answered the Lord: 'I am unworthy—how can I reply to you? I put my hand over my mouth. I spoke once, but I have no answer—twice, but I will say no more.'

"Then the Lord spoke to Job out of the storm: 'Brace yourself like a man; I will question you, and you shall answer me. Would you discredit my justice? Would you condemn me to justify yourself? Do you have an arm like God's, and can your voice thunder like his? Then adorn yourself with glory and splendor and clothe yourself in honor and majesty,'" and He goes on again for two more chapters.

Job had just been through an interrogation of sorts with God. But God was not angry with Job; He just wanted Job to understand what was in his heart. After this, Job's heart had changed, and he was finally able to answer God.

Job 42:1–6, "Then Job replied to the Lord: 'I know that you can do all things; no purpose of yours can be thwarted. You asked, "Who is this that obscures my plans without knowledge?" Surely, I spoke of things I did not understand, things too wonderful for me to know. You said, "Listen now, and I will speak; I will question you, and you shall answer me." My ears had heard of you but now my eyes have seen you. Therefore, I despise myself and repent in dust and ashes.'"

Job had finally realized it was not his own righteousness that mattered, but the Righteousness of God. His repentant heart with corresponding actions was all that God wanted to see in Job. God knew all along that the testing of Job's heart would prove his pure love, trust, and devotion to God at the end of his journey. And look next what God did for Job.

Job 40:10–17, "After Job had prayed for his friends, the Lord restored his fortunes and gave him twice as much as he had before. All his brothers and sisters and everyone who had known him before came and ate with him in his house. They comforted and consoled him over all the trouble the Lord had brought on him, and each one gave him a piece of silver and a gold ring. The Lord blessed the latter part of Job's life more than the former part. He had fourteen thousand sheep, six thousand camels, a thousand yoke of oxen and a thousand donkeys. And he also had seven sons and three daughters. The first daughter he named Jemimah, the second, Keziah, and the third, Keren-Happuch. Nowhere in all the land were there found women as beautiful as Job's daughters, and their father granted them an inheritance along with their brothers. After this, Job lived a hundred and forty years; he saw his children and their children to the fourth generation. And so, Job died, an old man and full of years."

Even in all this, Job was patient and endured through his sufferings. His perseverance to the end, even while God was teaching an amazing lesson on humility, brought him the most amazing reward. At the end of Job's incredible journey, God gave him *twice as much* as he had before, and he lived out the rest of his life blessed by God.

Romans 6:18 says, "Our present sufferings are not worth comparing with the glory that will be revealed in us."

Just as Job, many of us are going on with our normal, everyday lives when that sudden change in our circumstances takes place. And the first thing we want to know is, "Why God?" Maybe, we need to ask, "What God? What is Your purpose in the circumstance I'm facing?" Then trust Him with all our being that He is going to fulfil all that he intends and desires for each one of us. He has a plan. Will we allow him the opportunity to fulfil that plan the way He chooses?

I can tell you from my experience, from death to life, that it's worth it all!

Here I was, facing the closing of my own long journey that had begun just seven months earlier. I was about to go home, and I was reflecting back in my life.

It had been almost forty-three years to the day on Tuesday, June 6, 1972, that my wife was about ready to give birth. I was just waiting for those words, "I think it's time." All day, I had waited, and late that afternoon, I had to go to work. During my time at work, I had a difficult time keeping my mind focused on what needed to be done as I was thinking about the arrival of my first-born child entering into our newly formed family unit.

There was a false alarm that afternoon, as we felt the excitement of the anticipated arrival of our new baby but soon realized the disappointment that we would have to wait. It was almost unbearable.

Then, on the early hours of June 8, I heard those words out of a deep sleep, "I think it's time." Out of a stupor, I asked, "Time for what?" It wasn't long before we were on our way to the hospital, and our daughter was soon to be born. That afternoon, I went to the store to keep myself busy and purchased a roll of paper and paint. When I returned home, I made an eighteen-foot by three-foot sign that read, "WELCOME HOME SHAWNA." I hung it up above the sliding glass doors to welcome home my wife and my darling little baby girl. There's nothing like that kind of a welcome home.

Following a lengthy stay at the VA Hospital, the day I had longed for was finally here. I had been in and out of the hospital for months on end, and I couldn't wait to get home this time to stay. I wanted to see my bedroom, my bed, the front room, and the kitchen again; it was overwhelming. To smell the home-cooked meals, the scent of the house itself, was something I could only imagine. And this would be the day I was going to experience that glorious warm intimacy once again.

I would be driven home by my wife who had faithfully spent a few hours every day while I was in the hospital, sitting at my bedside, and at times, lying on the hospital bed next to me just snuggling up to me. But going home with her again was my ultimate desire.

I would lay in my hospital bed at night dreaming of that day. I could trace in my mind the layout of the house, and I would walk through every inch of it. All I would have to do is close my eyes, and I could picture it, imagining the feeling of being back in the comfort and security of our home. It's funny, but I could even remember the smell of my pillow. Oh, how I missed being home. The saying goes, "There's no place like home," and it is so very true.

After an extended time away, a person tends to forget about how exciting it is when they reconnect with their family and friends. Someone once said that distance makes the heart grow fonder.

As Melody and I pulled into the driveway and got out of the car, I paused just for a moment, as I anticipated what it was going to feel like when I first stepped into our home. As I walked up the nine stairs, with a cane and the help of my wife, I could hardly wait to make that connection again with my kids and my siblings. They had been so encouraging throughout my entire journey, and the love flowed between us.

When I entered through the door of our home, it was even more pleasant than I had imagined. Melody helped me get settled in my recliner in the living room, and all I could think was how life was going to be from now on.

I thought about when it would be time to go to bed that night. I had a memory foam mattress, and I couldn't wait to lie down on it. As the mattress would form to my body, it was going to feel like sheer ecstasy. And the home-cooked meals . . . no more hospital food! And being able to take baths instead of showers. I was looking forward to ending each day with a wonderful hot bath to totally unwind and relax.

I was still sitting in my recliner, listening to Melody in the kitchen. It sounded like she was starting to make dinner, as I could hear the clattering of pans and dishes. It wasn't long before I could smell the familiar home-cooked food. I was so happy to be home!

As I continued to relax, I couldn't help but think of what it's going to be like when we enter heaven, our eternal home. Coming home to an earthly home and the pleasure we get from that is only a mere taste of the glory it will be when we get to go home to heaven. I wondered, as I sat there, "What will it be like when our Heavenly Father says, 'Welcome home!'"

My thoughts raced back to when I died in the hospital, and I thought, "I could have been there right now," but apparently, He had another plan, and that plan included what I was experiencing in this moment. I was home with my wife and my family.

CHAPTER 22

From Spiritual Death to Spiritual Life

Have you ever wondered what heaven will be like? The Bible gives us a glimpse, and the following gives us a mental image of what awaits us after death.

Jesus told His disciples in John 14:2–3, "My Father's house has many rooms; if that were not so, would I have told you that I am going there to prepare a place for you? And if I go and prepare a place for you, I will come back and take you to be with me that you also may be where I am." What might those rooms or dwelling places look like? It's hard to envision.

Before His death, Jesus comforted his disciples with the promise that He would go and provide a place for them. The most beautiful part was His assurance that He would return for them and receive them unto Himself. Heaven will be breathtaking, but no matter how amazing the dwelling places in our Father's house, eternally abiding with Jesus will be the most beautiful environment of all.

A river, clear as crystal, will flow from the throne of God. It will run down the middle of the city. Can you even imagine it? On each side of the river, there will be a tree of life, producing twelve kinds of fruit every month. The streets will be pure gold, like transparent glass, and the walls of the city will be adorned with every kind of jewel, emerald, onyx, amethyst, topaz, etc. There will be no need for a sun or moon as the very presence of the Lord will be its light.

In the book of Revelation, the apostle John was privileged to see and report what heaven would be like. John witnessed in a vision that heaven possesses the "glory of God." As a matter of fact, Revelation 21:11 says, "It shone with the glory of God, and its brilliance was like that of a very precious jewel, like a jasper, clear as crystal," representing the very presence of God. Heaven will be a city filled with the brilliance of costly stones and crystal clear jasper.

Later on in Revelation 22:5, it says, "There will be no more night. They will not need the light of a lamp or the light of the sun, for the Lord God will give them light. And they will reign forever."

Then in Revelation 21:12–14, we're told that Heaven has twelve gates and twelve foundations. This will be the paradise of the Garden of Eden restored: the river of the water of life flows freely, and the tree of life is available once again, yielding fruit monthly with leaves that "heal the nations" Revelation 22:1–2.

It sounds amazing beyond anything we could ever imagine. But how can we know we'll get to go to heaven when we die? Is it something we can just hope for, or can we know?

My brother, Bruce, and I had attended a Good News Club one Thursday afternoon, August 16, in 1956. Margaret Hanson, who was the teacher, had just finished a flannel graph lesson when she asked if anyone would like to invite Jesus into their heart. She explained making Jesus your Savior was the only way a person could get to heaven. Since I had heard my mom and dad talk about that same thing on several occasions, and I'd heard it in Sunday School, I raised my hand in excitement.

We were meeting in the basement of her home in Bremerton, Washington, where she had a space cordoned off by some bed sheets. When we went forward to see how we could go to heaven, she took us behind one of the sheets that divided an area, separate from the room where she taught us.

She told us that what she would be saying was from the Bible and that we would be ready for heaven, as soon as we agreed, number one, that we had sinned. Well, that was an easy one, since I knew how I treated my little sister sometimes and also my brother. I also knew that sometimes, I lied to my parents. She turned in the Bible and read, "For all have sinned and fall short of the glory of God." Like I said, that was an easy one to agree to.

The second thing she told us was that because we had sinned, it would mean we would be separated from God when we died. This was a little harder to swallow, but she read from the Bible. "For the wages of sin is death."

Before we could wrap our heads around that one, she followed up with another more positive statement from the Bible which said, "But the gift of God is eternal life in Christ Jesus our Lord." So, if sinning would separate me from God but He had a gift that would eliminate that, what was I to do, how could I get that gift?

She kept going, "While we were still sinners, Christ died for us." She said that the only way we could be with God is if Jesus died for us so that we wouldn't be separated from Him.

Then she wrapped it up by reading from another two verses from the book of Romans, which said, "Everyone who calls on the name of the Lord will be saved." That word *saved* was the same word my mom and dad used when we talked about heaven.

She added, "If you declare with your mouth, 'Jesus is Lord,' and believe in your heart that God raised him from the dead, you will be saved." Even as a child, I understood what she was saying.

It was at that time she prayed with both my brother and me and both of us received Christ as our Savior and made heaven our eternal home.

The sin nature is that part of human beings that causes us to sin. The Bible teaches that we have a sin nature. Not only do we commit sin, but it is our nature to do so. This teaching is in contrast to that of many religious movements that deny original sin or total depravity. The sin nature is mentioned in several passages of Scripture. It is called the "earthly nature" in Colossians 3:15.

When God created Adam and Eve in the Garden of Eden, He called them *good,* along with the rest of His creation. They had no sin. However, their eating of the forbidden fruit had a devastating spiritual effect. Adam and Eve's children did not follow the *good* creation of God; in fact, the first child mentioned in Scripture, Cain, murdered his brother.

Seth, another child of Adam and Eve, was born with this sin nature as well. Genesis 5:3 notes, "When Adam had lived 130 years, he had a son in his own likeness, in his own image; and he named him Seth." Each person born since has likewise entered the world in the likeness of Adam, inheriting a sinful nature that begs redemption by God's grace.

In Psalm 51:5, David says, "Surely I was sinful at birth, sinful from the time my mother conceived me." David saw himself as a man whose sinful parents had brought forth a sinful child. David recognized that he possessed a nature that would sin and fall short of God's glory. David's son Solomon would later write that there is not a righteous man on earth who does good and never sins. Later in the book of Jeremiah, he comments on the sin nature: 'The heart is deceitful above all things and beyond cure."

The book of Romans offers the most complete look at the human condition. In Romans 5:12, Paul writes, "Therefore, just as sin entered the world through one man, and death through sin, and in this way, death came to all people, because all sinned." In other words, Adam's sin started it all, and now we are all sinners. Those who deny the sin nature are self-deceived. The unfortunate result of our sin nature is that we sin. Being sinners by nature, we cannot help but sin. These sins separate us from the perfect, sinless God.

Yet God has provided a way to receive forgiveness through Jesus Christ. Jesus spoke of salvation as being "born again." He told Nicodemus, "Very truly, I tell you, no one can enter the kingdom of God unless they are born of water and the Spirit. Flesh gives birth to flesh, but the Spirit gives birth to spirit. You should not be surprised at my saying, "You must be born again." John 3:5–7. Only Christ can overcome the sin nature within us. When a person trusts in Christ for salvation, he or she receives a new nature. The "natural man" becomes spiritual.

If you have never made Christ your Savior, and would like to, please pray this prayer

Dear Lord,

I admit that I am a sinner. I have done many things that don't please you. I have lived my life for myself only. I am sorry, and I repent. I ask you to forgive me.

I believe that you died on the cross for me, to save me. You did what I could not do for myself. I come to you now and ask you to take control of my life; I give it to you. From this day forward, help me to live every day for you and in a way that pleases you.

I love you, Lord, and I thank you that I will spend all eternity with you.

                                                  Amen.

When we repent, God forgives our sins and cleanses us from all unrighteousness. When we believe on His only begotten Son, Jesus as our Savior, He baptizes us into Christ, makes us a new creation, and the Spirit of Christ dwells in our heart (Romans 8:9). As we continue in the faith, read His Word, and grow in Him daily, He reveals Himself to us, shares His love, joy, peace, and life with us, and gives us victory over sin by the power of His Holy Spirit. If our faith endures to the end, God the Father will grant us an eternal inheritance with His Son Jesus.

Here's where our journey from spiritual death ends and our journey with spiritual life begins. Jesus desires that we *know* Him. Since we now have eternal life, we need to know what eternal life is. In John 17:3, it's explained to us, "After Jesus said this, he looked toward heaven and prayed: 'Father, the hour has come. Glorify your Son, that your Son may glorify you. For you granted him authority over all people that he might give eternal life to all those you have given him. *Now this is eternal life*: that they *know* you, the only true God, and Jesus Christ, whom you have sent."

But one might ask, "How can we *know* Jesus? How can we *know* God?" Well, think with me for a minute, how do we get to know each other? We have to spend time together, right? We have to *talk* to one another and *listen* to each other. Only, through communicating and being around someone can we get to know them. And it's the same in our relationship with Jesus.

He created us so that He could commune and fellowship with us. Revelation 3:20, "Here I am! I stand at the door and knock. If anyone hears my voice and opens the door, I will come in and eat with that person, and they with me." He is just waiting for our invitation. He's knocking at our heart's door, but it's up to us to open the door of our heart and allow Him to come in. That's not just the first time when we ask Him into our hearts to be our Savior. He wants full access to our hearts from that moment on.

How can we have that communion and fellowship with Him? First of all, we need to know that He desires for us to hear His voice. John 10:14–16, "I am the good shepherd; I know my sheep and my sheep know me—just as the Father knows me and I know the Father—and I lay down my life for the sheep. I have other sheep that are not of this sheep pen. I must bring them also. They too *will listen to my voice,* and there shall be one flock and one shepherd."

It may seem a little unfamiliar in the beginning. Think about how it might be when we receive a call from someone we just recently met; it takes a moment to recognize the voice because we're still unfamiliar with the sound of their voice. And sometimes, we even have to ask that person to identify themselves before we know who it is.

But on the other hand, when a family member or close friend calls, we recognize their voice and know immediately who it is without ever asking. It's the same way in our communication with Jesus. The more we listen to Him, through reading His Word and praying, we will soon *know it's Him* when He speaks.

This is where our new journey of spiritual life begins, in building a friendship with Jesus, simply by spending time with, talking to Him, and getting to know Him as we read His Word, the Bible. He wants to commune and fellowship with us, as well as, desiring that we commune and fellowship with Him. It's the most wonderful friendship ever! And the most fascinating journey we will ever travel!

In conclusion, here is the prayer Jesus prayed for us in John 17:4–26, "I have brought you glory on earth by finishing the work you gave me to do. And now, Father, glorify me in your presence with the glory I had with you before the world began."

Jesus Prays for His Disciples

I have revealed you to those whom you gave me out of the world. They were yours; you gave them to me and they have obeyed your word. Now they know that everything you have given me comes from you. For I gave them the words you gave me, and they accepted them. They knew with certainty that I came from you, and they believed that you sent me. I pray for them. I am not praying for the world, but for those you have given me, for they are yours. All I have is yours, and all you have is mine. And glory has come to me through them. I will remain in the world no longer, but they are still in the world, and I am coming to you. Holy Father protect them by the power of your name, the name you gave me, so that they may be one as we are one. While I was with them, I protected them and kept them safe by that name you gave me. None has been lost except the one doomed to destruction so that Scripture would be fulfilled.

 I am coming to you now, but I say these things while I am still in the world, so that they may have the full measure of my joy within them. I have given them your word and the world has hated them, for they are not of the world any more than I am of the world. My prayer is not that you take them out of the world but that you protect them from the evil one. They are not of the world, even as I am not of it. Sanctify them by the truth; your word is truth. As you sent me into the world, I have sent them into the world. For them I sanctify myself, that they too may be truly sanctified.

Jesus Prays for All Believers

My prayer is not for them alone. I pray also for those who will believe in me through their message, that all of them may be one, Father, just as you are in me and I am in you. May they also be in us so that the world may believe that you have sent me. I have given them the glory that you gave me, that they may be one as we are one—I in them and you in me—so that they may be brought to complete unity. Then the world will know that you sent me and have loved them even as you have loved me.

Father, I want those you have given me to be with me where I am, and to see my glory, the glory you have given me because you loved me before the creation of the world.

"Righteous Father, though the world does not know you, I know you, and they know that you have sent me. I have made you known to them and will continue to make you known in order that the love you have for me may be in them and that I myself may be in them.

APPENDIX

When I entered the VA hospital in mid-January of 2015, I didn't expect to spend so much time there. The doctors and nurses were very friendly and conversational, which made me feel like I was being treated with the utmost care. I also didn't realize that they were recording everything, including statements that I made.

When I was finally released, I went back and requested my medical records. I waited in the area in front of the medical records department. It was a long wait, and I thought that they were really busy. After a while, I approached the window and asked if I should come back. The lady behind the counter said that it would take a long time to copy all the records. After another wait, she returned with a box full of papers. It was my records on three thousand pages. I didn't expect that.

As I read through everything that was documented, I found some interesting remarks that I had made but had forgotten.

The following are a few examples

On January 16, 2015, at 6:00 a.m. "I believe in the Lord." Previous to that comment, it stated that I was pleasant but in poor health.

On another occasion, six days later, "Veteran and his family trust deeply in God. They believe that God is sovereign over all things and that all things happen according to God's perfect plan. They do not believe anything "bad" will happen, even though it may feel unpleasant, because they believe all things happen according to God's purpose for good. Veteran served as a minister for twenty-four years, including two years as a missionary to the land of Korea."

On April 18, a nurse had logged in that the "Veteran wondered aloud what God is doing in the midst of it all. Veteran reported that he has a twenty-four-year history in the ministry but did not elaborate on his experience. Veteran spoke of his belief that God is with him and somehow at work in his life.

It was also noted at this time that my "Spiritual disciplines included prayer, reading, and studying the Scripture."

Some of the scriptures that sustained my family and me through this whole ordeal and gave credence to our faith are as follows:

Hebrews 13:5, "I will never, under any circumstances, desert you nor give you up nor leave you without support, nor will I in any degree leave you helpless, nor will I forsake *or* let you down *or* relax My hold on you assuredly not!"

Deuteronomy 31:8, "It is the Lord who goes before you; He will be with you. He will not fail you or abandon you. Do not fear or be dismayed."

Genesis 50:20, "As for you, you meant evil against me, but God meant it for good in order to bring about this present outcome, that many people would be kept alive, as they are this day. 'Speaking to Satan I would say, "You intended to harm me, but God intended it all for good. He brought me to this position. So, I could save the lives of many people."

Isaiah 41:10, "'Do not fear anything, for I am with you; Do not be afraid, for I am your God. I will strengthen you, be assured I will help you; I will certainly take hold of you with My righteous right hand a hand of justice, of power, of victory, of salvation."

Psalms 118:23–24, "This is from the Lord *and* is His doing; It is marvelous in our eyes. This day in which God has saved me is the day which the Lord has made; Let us rejoice and be glad in it."

Psalms 118:17, "I will not die, but live, and declare the works *and* recount the illustrious acts of the Lord."

Proverbs 3:5, "Trust in *and* rely confidently on the Lord with all your heart and do not rely on your own insight *or* understanding."

2 Corinthians 1:10, "He rescued us from so great a *threat of* death and will *continue to* rescue us. On Him we have set our hope. And He will again rescue us from danger and draw us near."

Psalms 118:23, 24, "This is from the Lord *and* is His doing; It is marvelous in our eyes."

Psalms 119:37–38, "Turn my eyes away from vanity, all those worldly, meaningless things that distract—let Your priorities be mine and restore me with renewed energy in Your ways. Establish Your word *and* confirm Your promise to Your servant, as that which produces awe-inspired reverence for You."

Psalms 119:154, "Plead my cause and redeem me; revive me *and* give me life according to the promise of Your word."

Psalms 119:159, "Consider how I love Your precepts; revive me *and* give me life, O Lord, according to Your loving kindness."

ABOUT THE AUTHOR

Bud Kolstad has served in ministry during most of his adult life and is retired from the pastorate of twenty-four years, including serving two years as a missionary in Korea. He is a graduate of Pacific Coast Baptist Bible College and a Biola University alumni. In the recent years that followed his college education, he became a syndicated columnist in northern California, in addition to pastoring.

He has a passion for discipleship and is gifted in teaching Godly principles for spiritual development. Currently, he is involved in teaching small-group discipleship classes in his local church. His desire is to see believers grasp on to the truths in God's Word, moving them toward a more intimate relationship with Jesus Christ, and growing into spiritual maturity.

He is a husband, the father of three children, and the grandfather of ten grandchildren. He currently resides in the northwest with his wife and family.

ABOUT THE CO-AUTHOR

Jill Cromwell is a wife, mother, grandmother, and writer. She is a published author, with the release of her first book, *The Tapestry God's Masterpiece*. She has enjoyed years of journaling, which has been the inspiration for her love of writing. Her passion is seeing people *grow through* life events as she believes that everything serves a purpose and believes no experience should be wasted. She has a creative perspective on how God will take even the bad things in our lives and turn them into something good if we will let Him.

Throughout her forty-five-year spiritual journey, Jill has taught women's Bible studies, group Bible studies, children's ministries, along with serving in leadership positions both in ministry, as well as her career. She and her husband served as staff members in their local church in Arizona, pioneering a benevolence ministry that served thousands of individuals within that community.

Jill and her husband are currently residing in the southern panhandle of Texas along with their family.

CPSIA information can be obtained
at www.ICGtesting.com
Printed in the USA
BVHW062222131218
535379BV00001B/4/P